Praise for
DELIGHT IN THE LIMELIGHT

"Linda Ugelow is a champion for those who suffer from public speaking anxiety. In *Delight in the Limelight*, she offers a fresh approach to transform that fear from the inside out."
MICHAEL PORT, *New York Times-* and *Wall Street Journal-*bestselling author of *Steal the Show* and *The Referable Speaker*

"It would be easy to just treat the symptom of camera-fright, and, in fact, that's what most books and coaches do. Thankfully, Linda Ugelow goes far deeper than that with this wonderful and practical book. She helps you not only find and heal the source of your fears but also build the skills and frameworks for you to finally become the speaker and presenter you want to be."
TAMSEN WEBSTER, author of *Find Your Red Thread*

"I love this book! It is wise, passionate, grounded, and immensely practical. Using a wide range of wonderful stories and powerful, actionable techniques, Linda Ugelow shows us how to access our best selves, and gives us the tools to speak in public with freedom and joy. If you're nervous about public speaking, or if you simply want to experience the power of integrating your authentic self into your professional life, this book is for you."
REBECCA M. HENDERSON, author of *Reimagining Capitalism in a World on Fire*

"'Fear is not the villain. It's the messenger.' From that line, I was hooked. Linda Ugelow helps you get the message and then act upon it. Her Inner Freedom Framework will change the way you see your fear and yourself. And that could change your life."

HEATHER HANSEN, author of *The Elegant Warrior* and *Advocate to Win*

"Whether you get butterflies when you speak or perhaps avoid presentation opportunities altogether, this book is the ultimate roadmap for overcoming anxiety onstage or on camera. Step up and let your voice be heard!"

DORIE CLARK, author of *Stand Out* and executive education faculty, Duke University's Fuqua School of Business

"*Delight in the Limelight* expertly guides you to overcome your public speaking fears and thrive in the spotlight. A must-read for anyone who wants to shine onstage or on camera."

PAULA RIZZO, media strategist, Emmy Award–winning television producer, bestselling author of *Listful Living*

"Finally, someone who can show me not how to mask fear when I'm speaking, but to skip it altogether! We're so lucky Linda Ugelow captured her message about being naturally 'you' onstage and in front of the camera."

LAURA BELGRAY, founder of Talking Shrimp and author of *Tough Titties*

"*Delight in the Limelight* will show you how to be the best 'you,' onstage or off. Hint: You don't need to change a thing, just channel who you already are."

MIKE MICHALOWICZ, bestselling author of *Get Different* and *Profit First*

"We all crave self-expression—and yet, for so many of us, that urge to speak competes with our anxiety and dread of being seen. We're often told to shrug off our fear so we can 'crush it' onstage. What Linda Ugelow offers is a far more thoughtful and effective framework for approaching the stage or the screen. *Delight in the Limelight* is a must-have guide for anyone who's ever felt their soul drain out of their bodies at the mere thought of stepping up to the podium. When you follow Linda's lead, you won't just temporarily tamp down panic, you will heal its painful root so that you can stop cowering in the shadows and begin to blossom in the attention of others."

TERRI TRESPICIO, writer, speaker, and author of *Unfollow Your Passion*

"Linda Ugelow's message is so needed in the speaking industry. I've been a professional writing coach at some of the most high-end speaking programs in the world and I've seen people follow every piece of advice, framework, trick, and tip to overcome their fear—only to be disappointed. This book is courageous enough to talk about what's really behind stage fright and how to finally overcome it. One of the most important books about public speaking."

CLEMENTINA ESPOSITO, founder, The Clementina Collective

"For anyone who fears public speaking, Linda Ugelow's approach will come as a welcome relief. Instead of shame, punishment, and force, she comes from a place of love and understanding. Let her wisdom guide you to speak with freedom and ease."

HELENA BOWEN, speaker coach and speechwriter

DELIGHT *in the* LIMELIGHT

Overcome Your Fear of Being Seen and Realize Your Dreams

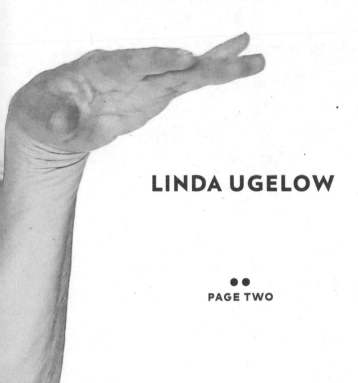

LINDA UGELOW

●●
PAGE TWO

Some names and identifying details have been changed to protect
the privacy of individuals.

This book is not intended as a substitute for the medical advice
of physicians. The reader should regularly consult a physician in
matters relating to his/her health and particularly with respect to
any symptoms that may require diagnosis or medical attention.

Cataloguing in publication information is available from
Library and Archives Canada.
ISBN 978-1-98960-394-9 (paperback)
ISBN 978-1-98960-395-6 (ebook)
ISBN 978-1-77458-141-4 (audiobook)

Page Two
pagetwo.com

Edited by AJ Harper and Amanda Lewis
Copyedited by Steph VanderMeulen
Proofread by JoAnne Burek and Alison Strobel
Cover and interior design by Jennifer Lum
Author photos by Caroline White Photography
Printed and bound in Canada by Friesens
Distributed in Canada by Raincoast Books
Distributed in the US and internationally by Macmillan

21 22 23 24 25   5 4 3 2 1

LindaUgelow.com

CONTENTS

To the speaker inside waiting to be set free

> *"The more scared we are of a work or calling,*
> *the more sure we can be that we have to do it."*
> **STEVEN PRESSFIELD**

INTRODUCTION

Y EARS AGO, I abandoned a big dream.

As a child, all I ever wanted to do was dance. At eighteen I took a class in dance/movement therapy and was impassioned to make a societal impact by turning people onto the magic of dance and creating communities of dancing divas. The classes I led were creative and fun, and I connected with a few incredible souls. But I knew squat about business and marketing, and after twenty years of furtively posting flyers on bulletin boards and streetlamp poles, I gave up the dream.

This is what I told myself: "Who was I to think I was so important that what I had to share was worthwhile or any better than someone else? That's just being grandiose, right?" And besides, I just didn't have it in me to know how to go about being a person of impact.

After fifteen years of wandering in the proverbial career desert, I finally discovered a new passion in organic farming, and I created a business growing specialty vegetables for local restaurants. I loved to see itty bitty seeds sprout out of the soil and become yellow tomatoes with red streaks or tender-leaved baby collards. It was an introvert's paradise to tend a small farm—for a few years.

One day, I sat on the ground to weed around the onions and listen to a course module from online business coach Marie Forleo on how to start the right business. Suddenly I shot to my feet. *Being a farmer is kinda cool,* I thought, *but it's not what I'm meant to do.* I wanted to make an impact, grandiose or not, and here I was playing small, hiding behind the kale.

At that moment, I made a decision. I would become an online entrepreneur. I had no idea exactly what I would do or how I would get there, but one thing was clear: if I reached the end of my life and I hadn't seen what I was capable of, I would be filled with regret. As I looked over the fields and woods in the distance, I felt the call of a hero's journey.

Do you dream of greatness? Do you have a secret fantasy or vision of your personal impact at work or as an entrepreneur that could move you into a whole new sphere of influence? If you never let the secret speaker out, will you get to the end of your life filled with regret?

Jeannie was a risk-taker. Out of school, she sold everything she owned, moved to Los Angeles, where she didn't know a soul, and got work as a playwright. She discovered a favorite cafe and spent her days writing there along with other Hollywood creatives. One of them, a screenwriter, became a close friend.

At the time, Jeannie was obsessed with a certain hour-long TV drama. Absolutely obsessed. As fate would have it, this particular friend knew many of the writers for that show and generously offered to set up a meeting between Jeannie and the writers. He asked her to prepare a pitch for a potential storyline for the show. What serendipity, right? It was a dream come true!

The day came. Jeannie didn't go to the meeting. She was just too terrified. Decades later, full of regret, she still wonders how her life would have unfolded had she been able to show up and share her ideas that day.

I don't want that to happen to you. I don't want you to give up on your dream because you are afraid to be seen. Nor do I want you to live with regret.

Have you ever watched others take the stage and yearned to be that person? Or have you dreamed of the opportunities and recognition that would come your way if only you could get yourself to regularly make videos or speak at your local chamber of commerce or represent your team at work? Do you wish you could just feel confident and at ease when all eyes are on you?

Your dream *can* come true. You can be that person onstage, unafraid. You can shine on camera. You can feel better and more confident about your speaking than you ever imagined. I'm not saying this in a "rah-rah" motivational way. I really believe it's possible. You can transform the fear and learn to love being in the limelight.

I know this is true because of how I was able to make this transformation myself, and quickly, too, after decades of suffering.

Back in grad school, before I found a career as a farmer, I created an independent study in the Expressive Therapies program and researched a practice called Authentic Movement. It's like a cross between stream-of-consciousness and movement meditation.

Here it is in a nutshell: You, as the mover, close your eyes and "listen" for an impulse to move your body, and give permission to let it happen. The movement inevitably morphs into something new, and you let that happen too. It's as if you let your body speak in its own language of movement and your mind simply follows along with keen interest, fascination even, as you notice the sensations, your emotions and mental associations. It's kind of like being in a trance or high on something. I thought it was totally cool.

My advisor, Marion, in her sincere desire to support me in my passion, suggested I give a presentation about it. We'd invite professors from the various Expressive Therapies departments: drama, music, art, and dance.

I was flattered by her suggestion. It sounded so grown up and important. The only problem was, I had never given a talk and had no idea how to go about it. I definitely did not know how to plan for one. So, I didn't plan. I figured I'd improvise what I wanted to say in the moment.

As the room filled with important people, my body began to shake and tremble. And when I stood up to speak, I discovered to my horror that the saliva in my mouth had completely vanished and been replaced by cotton. I never knew my mouth could feel so totally dry.

I opened my mouth to speak, but nothing came out. More than anything, I wanted to crawl inside a hole. But I valiantly stood there and tried again. Still no sound.

I opened and closed my mouth like a fish.

Marion leaned forward and whispered, "Linda, would you like a glass of water?"

What a godsend! The water gave me back my sound, but my brain never recovered. I rambled and stumbled along until the ordeal was finally over.

I don't remember what I said that day. I only recall feeling deeply embarrassed and ready to crawl under the covers.

After that mortification I stayed "under the covers" as far as public speaking was concerned for a decade, and it was still another fifteen years after that before I finally discovered how to overturn my anxiety so I could not just get up to speak, but even enjoy the process.

I'm eternally grateful for that pivotal moment because that's what brought me to write this book: I don't want you to waste your precious time fearing public speaking, like I did. Today I work with entrepreneurs, employees, and executives to transform their trepidation of public speaking, whether on camera or to a live audience. How I did it, how they did it, and how you can, too, is the subject of this book.

When we hear the word "speaker," we tend to picture a person on a stage or behind a podium. Today, though, speaking is not limited to these settings. Speaking platforms have grown with our ever-expanding technology to include video, livestreaming, webinars, tele-summits, podcasts, TV, and more.

Anyone who chooses to can spread their message on a bigger scale, to make connections and influence the conversation. If you want to be part of that and you're holding back, you're missing out.

But it's not just what you miss out on that's at stake here. It's also what other people miss out on. Because Jeannie was unable to get over her fear, her would-be fans missed out on the amazing stories she would create.

And this goes for you too. If you're not getting out there, think about all the people who can't get your help, inspiration, or perspective. You owe it to them and to yourself to be visible.

You may rather tweet your way into leadership, or get credit at work for the behind-the-scenes support you provide. You may wish to create impact with a book or a blog. Ah, but here's the catch. These days, a book needs to be promoted. If your blog draws a big following, you'll be asked to speak.

There's nothing as impressive or compelling as showing your face, as being seen and heard. Why? Because if someone is going to follow you or buy from you, whether that's onstage, on camera, or in the meeting room, they want to get a broader sense of you, your voice, your personality, and your energy. When you speak at the front of the room, it gives you instant credibility. Your face on camera shows you as a leader.

The term "limelight" reaches back to nineteenth-century theater lighting. Contrary to immediate word associations, it has nothing to do with fruit or the color green. In those pre-electricity times, a chunk of limestone or calcium was heated to a brilliant white glow that could be beamed onto the stage. Those standing in the limelight could be seen by the audience.

I want you to be seen by your audience. The enormous opportunity that is available right now to put your personal stamp on humanity cannot be overestimated. On a societal level, we are being called to speak up and speak out. And I believe we need more voices to join in on the important conversations of our lives. We need the voices of people looking to make our families and communities better, kinder, and healthier. In particular, the world needs those who have historically been silenced, discouraged, and dismissed to stand up. I want to empower you to discover your confidence, ease, and joy. Because if you are reading this book, I know you feel tapped on the shoulder to make a contribution, and that you have a unique personal perspective that your team, business, clients, and customers need.

You are actually already a speaker in the limelight. You speak throughout your day, at the grocery store, on the telephone, to neighbors on the street, friends, family, and colleagues.

We speak to influence and persuade, to share knowledge and new ideas, to inspire, lead, and motivate. We speak to draw our community around us and build relationships with them, to build our brands, our businesses, our thought leadership, to solve problems and have fun. But as speakers, we feel comfortable in some situations, but not in others; speaking to some groups of people, but not other groups; to a certain number of people, but not another number.

Regardless of where you're at, I'm going to teach you not only how to survive public speaking, but also how to delight in the limelight.

I want you to feel unlimited. To not be held back by discomfort or fear, by inhibition and limiting beliefs. I want you to lean into the opportunities to expand into your full potential that visibility provides. I want speaking to be one of your happy places. I want it to feel fun, to be one of the best things you get to do. Because life's too short for things that don't bring us joy.

This book is for:

- Online entrepreneurs who recognize the advantages and power of the camera to attract and build their audience but can't get past the fear of appearing so publicly.

- Authors who want to not only write books but also get their book into readers' hands and engage with their fans.

- The C-suite executive who secretly dreads presentations, made worse by their difficulty in showing vulnerability and owning up to their fears because their position comes with the expectation that they have it all together.

- Corporate leaders and team players who want to be noticed, move up the corporate ladder, and be paid what they're worth.

- Artists and changemakers who want to bring attention to their work or cause and persuade and influence others, but who feel that speaking is outside their comfort zone and area of expertise.

- The experienced keynoter or presenter who silently suffers from nerves and anxiety each time they get in front of their audience. They have resigned themselves to their fear, assuming it comes with the territory of speaking, and do the best they can to manage it.

I'm here to help you.

If you feel trepidation when you step into the limelight, I want to honor that. Others would advise you to "feel the fear and do it anyway." I won't do that here.

If you are concerned about being judged, looking the fool, ruining your reputation, and being rejected, I honor those feelings. Because there was probably a time in your life when these things happened, when you were judged, felt foolish, or embarrassed, or not good enough.

What makes this book different from other books on the fear of public speaking is the approach that fear is a symptom of something deeper, a root cause of fear that you need to address to move forward. I don't want you to just take a pill and mask the emotion. I want to uncover what is behind or beneath the fear and solve for that. When you look at fear from this perspective, with curiosity and compassion, you will discover the fastest, deepest, most transformative process I know of to overcome the fear. You will not push past or manage the fear, but rather face, embrace, and erase the fear by getting to the root of it and make real change. Fast.

How fast?

You may imagine that it takes a long time to go from feeling like you're about to pass out on the spot to standing with confidence and ease. After all, you've most likely been fearful of or avoided the camera or public speaking for years, if not decades. It may surprise you, then, to learn that the average number of private sessions I have with my clients is only six to eight. Students make their way through my self-directed speaking confidence program in a similar amount of time.

That's much shorter than the time it takes to perfect a golf swing or learn to stand on your head in yoga. And although those will give you a sense of satisfaction and empowerment, overcoming your fear of speaking in public will have enormous implications on where you end up in life.

This book is right for you if

- you are tired of playing small,

- you feel like the best-kept secret,

- you would later regret having avoided opportunities,

- you would love to utilize today's amazing ways to teach and spread your message, and/or

- you want to expand into your full potential and see what you are capable of.

What waits for you on the other side of fear?

Instead of looking for the exit when opportunities knock, imagine saying yes! Rather than dreading a speaking opportunity and looking forward to it being over, imagine excitement and delight as you look out at your audience. Instead of self-consciousness and awkwardness, imagine a sense of joyful self-expression in front of the camera lens. Imagine the satisfaction of having a platform where you share your ideas and impact people's lives for the better.

This book will not tell you what to say or how to say it. (There are plenty of good books already written on the topic, and I share some of my favorites in the bibliography.) Rather, it's about how to transform your willingness to get up in front of people or in front of the lens and how to create the best experience for yourself. It will guide you into experiencing your power and strength, your free expression, and your delight in being seen and heard.

Once you've dealt with fear, it's done. But feeling freely and naturally yourself is a work in progress. With the help of this book, which I've designed to walk you through your transformation, you'll discover how to make this a joyful process.

Along this journey, you'll meet up with loving friends and guides of the best kind. You'll be given the tools to help you re-chart your personal map. You will be asked to call upon your skills and capabilities, to widen your senses, intuition, and the powers of your imaginative mind. You'll invite your body's intelligence and sensibility to support you. It will be fun. Or at least interesting. And who knows? The process may be quicker than you think.

I want you to find a new inner experience of what you think is possible for yourself. If you cover all the material in the book, I believe this will happen for you, just as it has for me and countless clients with whom I've had the honor to work.

Whether you've never spoken up before or you're a seasoned keynoter who manages your anxiety before every appearance, if you sense that you are meant to play on a bigger stage, by the end of this book you will have what you need to put yourself in the spotlight without dread or fear. You'll experience a shift in your perspective that will change your experience of the limelight, yourself, and your business for the better.

Are you ready to get started? Let's go!

1

Practice Is Not a Panacea for Getting Over Fear

"Your task is not to seek for love, but merely to seek and find all the barriers within yourself that you have built against it."

RUMI

YOU WANT TO and you don't want to.

You wish you could and you wish you didn't have to.

You dream of it and dread it.

"Do you feel scared, too? When do you stop feeling nervous?" These were the questions I asked my video mentor Holly Gillen, who introduced me to livestreaming on the Periscope app.

Her response? "Everybody says by seventy-five days, you'll feel fine."

"Seventy-five?" Oh man! I braced myself.

I had just begun my first week of livestreaming on Periscope (now defunct), an app that people from around the world could hop on to see what you were up to. I saw this then new platform as a way to become known in my coaching business. The first Periscope rock stars got their following by "going live" every single day. That was my plan too.

The only problem was, just the act of opening my notebook to jot down my talking points brought on an attack of nerves. My heart pounded hard. A second wave of fear blasted as I pressed the broadcast button. Finally, after a couple of minutes on live, I'd calm down.

Each day, I pushed toward that magic number of seventy-five and tried to manage my nerves in all the ways I could think of—deep breathing, jumping jacks, dancing to music, power poses. When I ran out of ideas, I googled how to get over stage fright. I reframed my nerves as excitement. (As if I can't feel the difference between fear and excitement, ha!) I told myself, *It's not about me, it's about the audience. That fear was fuel to get energized.*

I gobbled up all the heroic messages on fear posted on social media.

"Ignore the fear, don't let it hold you back."

"The magic happens outside your comfort zone."

"Feel the fear and do it anyway."

"If you're not scared, you're not taking enough risks."

I joined a Periscope cheerleader squad whose anthem was #DoItScared. I was grateful for a team of brave women with whom I could feel solidarity. I was a total believer in "doing it scared" and pushing through the fear, because, well, I didn't know there was an alternative. I mean, some people were naturally happy in the limelight and others were not, right? Some people get off on the adrenaline rush of roller coasters and Ferris wheels and maybe enjoy the same rush when they stand in front of the lens.

At this point, you may think that I'm going to show you ways to muscle up to the other side. Nope. As I mentioned earlier, I'm not going to do that. I'm not here to tell you to just get over it. Or to ignore it. Or that it's just a misperception in your head. Or to pretend that fear is the same as excitement—as if you don't know the difference, too. After all, if "getting over it" were that easy, you would have done it already, and I wouldn't need to write this book.

Look, I'm not here to bash courage. We do absolutely need to be brave at times. Sometimes we have no choice. Life will surprise us with curveballs, when we need to summon our moral, physical, or emotional courage. But do we really want to live feeling afraid? And more than that, if we wear our fear as a badge of honor, do we unwittingly chain ourselves to it?

Here is what I didn't know back when I was "doing it scared": *Fear is not the villain. It's the messenger.* Just as pain in your body tells you to pay attention, fear wants your attention too. It says, "Look over here!" Most people respond to both fear and pain with a management strategy. They look for a quick solution that takes the edge off.

Managing fear, though, is not the same as dissolving fear. Just as managing pain is not the same as dissolving the need for your body to be in pain. For instance, you could take ibuprofen for a frozen shoulder, but that just minimizes the pain. It doesn't deal with why the pain is there in the first place. If you don't take care of the root cause, you never get over the pain, you just manage it. Likewise, you can take beta-blocker for your anxiety, but that doesn't eliminate the fear. It simply masks it for a while.

Stage fright isn't just something we make up. It's our body's innate response to fear. And it's highly distracting! When you have sweaty hands and your legs shake, it's hard to pay attention to anything else! That means less mental bandwidth to remember what you want to say, and less capacity to be present with your audience. It means less chance to feel freely self-expressive, let alone to have fun.

Fear puts your body in a state of fight, flight, or freeze. When you feel fearful, a part of your brain called the amygdala shuts down access to another part of your brain, the prefrontal cortex, affecting your concentration and memory. Yes, that's why your brain goes blank when you feel put on the spot.

The bottom line with *managing* fear is that, ultimately, it doesn't *get rid of* the fear. In fact, for most people, the longer you push through fear, the longer it will take to get over it. You may become a good performer, but your inner experience will not match the outer. Pushing through fear is good as a short-term solution to get the deed done. But if you really want to get *over* your fear for good, you need to slow down, look at it with curiosity, and see what it's made of.

My "Duh" Moment

Day seventy-five of my daily Periscopes arrived. My finger hovered over the broadcast button as my heart pounded painfully in my chest. I pressed my lips firmly together and then froze. *Wait a second!* I thought. *I've been in battle with my fear every day. Has it disappeared? No!* I still felt like I would collapse of a heart attack. I hadn't become the cool, confident livestreamer I had hoped to be.

And on this particular day, I saw the reality. I was showing up, getting better at livestreaming and building an audience, but the fear wasn't going away.

"I hate how this feels," I pouted. "What can I do to get rid of this?"

I ran through my personal resources. I reminded myself that I was a performer, a movement specialist (with a master's degree, no less), and a mindset coach with years of personal development and experimentation. I might know a thing or two about this stuff. I sat myself down and asked (yes, I talk to myself like this), *If someone came to you, Linda, about feeling nervous in front of the camera, what would you do to help them?*

I made a long list of ideas on a clean sheet in my notebook. Where to start? One on the list popped out—a technique called Focusing that brings your attention into your body to discover information—for example: "Before I try to get rid of this fear, what is this fear even about? What does it feel like?"

I closed my eyes and leaned into my fear. What was it trying to say? What came back was, *I'm going to be attacked.* I pondered this. *Attacked? Could this be an ancestral memory coded into my DNA, like fear of the saber-toothed tiger?* Perhaps, but I looked back to my childhood. I had, in fact, been attacked on a number of occasions. Typically, by my two older sisters who would charge at me, kick my shins, and call me stupid.

Here's the real kicker, though (pun intended). My sisters attacked me whenever I got special attention from our mom attention they craved but only I received, because I was the "good" girl and they were naughty.

"Why can't you girls be like Linda?" Mom would ask them. That was their cue to attack. After she left the room, of course.

I realized I didn't feel safe in front of the camera, or speaking to an audience, because there was a part of me that remembered *being the center of attention was dangerous.* My sisters hated me for the attention I received and attacked me out of jealousy.

I resisted this conclusion at first. My sisters and I grew out of that stage long ago, and we've been great friends ever since. Yet somehow it rang true. I double-checked to see if I still felt that risk. I asked my body, "Am I afraid that my sisters wouldn't love me anymore if I were successful in my work, if I got too much attention?"

Yes, I'm still afraid of losing their love.

Somehow, even though it was long, long ago, the imprint of that time was still with me.

There's probably a good reason why you fear the limelight. Fear doesn't exist in a vacuum. It's not a random emotion without a cause. If you don't like people to look at you, most likely there was a time in your past when you learned it wasn't safe. Maybe that came from what your parents said or did (or didn't say or do), or your teachers or classmates, or something you were taught to believe. If you worry that you'll be judged or hurt or rejected, you probably were judged, hurt, or rejected, or maybe you saw it happen to somebody else.

We don't start out this way. Think of the toddler who pulls themselves up on their feet and takes their first tentative steps. If the people around delight in this accomplishment, the child is thrilled to be the cause of joy and undeterred in being wholly themselves.

We do our best to adapt. To follow the rules. To keep ourselves in the good graces of those bigger and more powerful around us. To fit in and be likable by our friends and peers. We do what we need to protect ourselves. We use the resources that we have at our disposal. That might mean to become quiet, or to retreat into our own world, to be a behind-the-scenes kind of person, or to freely express ourselves only with a small circle of friends or alone in our room.

Over time, what we use to protect ourselves gradually becomes who we think we are—shy, self-conscious, inhibited, nervous that what happened before might happen again, even when we have no conscious memory of it.

You might think that all the circumstances from your past are long gone, that what happened then is no longer a big deal or doesn't impact you. But every time you feel fear as you stand in front of the camera or a crowd, it's because unbeknownst to you, you're dragging around a conglomeration of memories and conclusions about what it takes to be safe. And because it's so familiar, you maybe don't notice that this rope is tied to your ankle and goes wherever you go.

This is why you freak out when someone pulls out their phone and says, "Let's make a video," or why you feel like you're going to vomit before you walk out onstage. This is why you avoid making videos for your website even though you know a great video of you there would increase your customers and influence. This is why you turn down opportunities for leadership positions. This is why when you do present, you tremble, even if nobody else can tell.

If you really want to get over your fear, don't look at fear as something to get past without examination. Rather, open yourself to your innate curiosity about your most cherished topic—*you!* Take time to explore and unravel your life, your thoughts and feelings about how you present yourself to the world.

The process of self-discovery that developed from that one question—what does the fear want to say?—completely changed my experience of the camera lens. The lens no longer triggered fear; rather, it centered presence. It triggered a sense of calm focus and joy. Can I say how freakin' excited I was to be on the other side of fear?

I noticed a big shift when I performed with my women's world music group too. Although I already felt relaxed and open to dancing or singing, I used to dread if I had to introduce the next number. Now, I noticed a new response. I thought, *Oh, good, it's my turn to speak!*

My confidence to apply for other opportunities opened up. I presented at the European Conference of Positive Psychology in France, co-directed and presented a video for *Money Magazine* in New York City, and was emcee for TEDxDebrecenUniversity in Hungary. For fun, I began storytelling at local slams. Most significantly, I began to work with others to help them achieve this same comfort and ease that they desired when they stepped into the limelight.

When people come to me for help, it's often after they've tried lots of other programs to make videos or become a speaker, programs that helped them with what to say but didn't eliminate their fear. That's because scripts will give you what to say and practice takes away the fear of not being prepared, but the fear of being unprepared is different from the fear of being seen and heard. That's why you can find numerous performers and speakers who are highly skilled, highly prepared, highly regarded, and highly paid and who still have to manage their stress and nerves.

Many of my clients use the term "inner freedom" to describe how it feels to be on the other side of fear. This is why I call the process that I take people through to overcome their fear and delight in the limelight the Inner Freedom Framework. The framework takes you through three main processes.

First, you investigate the fear to reveal and heal the root causes.

Second, you restore a sense of safety inside and look at how to create safety in your environment.

Third, you repattern your habits. You swap out the old ways of holding tension, using your voice and expressing yourself in new ways that are aligned in how you want to feel and be seen. Rather than push fear away, ignore it, or punch it in the face, let's summon our courage to face it and embrace it.

Beneath the Fear

Fear has a primary purpose: to protect you. Fear keeps you safe from harm, rejection, and ridicule. So, let's honor it for the good job that it does.

Fear is also a gift. It gives you the opportunity to open yourself to the next level of your evolution and fulfillment. It's only when your ambivalence and limitations impede the manifestation of your desires that you have the motivation to change or seek a solution.

Throughout this book, you'll come across ideas you'll want to journal about to help you work through the material. I suggest you keep that journal handy so that as thoughts are triggered, you can capture them on the page. To make it easy, I've created a fillable one that goes along with this book. To download it, as well as other resources that support you on your speaking journey, go to delightinthe limelight.com/resources.

You may also want to invite a friend or create a small group to go on this journey with you. This companionship serves several functions. It provides structure and accountability and builds intimacy and community. Shared experience is healing unto itself and makes the process all the more fun.

For accountability, email me at linda@lindaugelow.com to share that you've begun your journey to speaking confidence. Put in the subject line, "I'm starting my journey to delight in the limelight" and tell me you are committed to discovering your speaking confidence. I'm serious. Send me an email. I want to know that you've begun.

I'm honored to travel alongside you. I'll be rooting for you.

START WITH THIS

Pull out your journal and write down your top three or four goals for yourself as a result of reading this book and implementing the teachings.

Examples:

- "I'll feel energized and excited about speaking in front of people."

- "I'll no longer dread making videos."

- "I'll feel more accepting of my mistakes."

- "I'll finally get rid of the nervousness and nausea before stepping out onstage."

Think about what life will be like for you on the other side of fear. What are you doing? How do you feel? How do you look? What do people say about you?

If you think it will inspire you, grab a photo of an energetic, confident, engaging speaker to whom you relate; make a vision board; or sketch how you and your confident life will look.

THE INNER
FREEDOM FRAMEWORK

PART 1

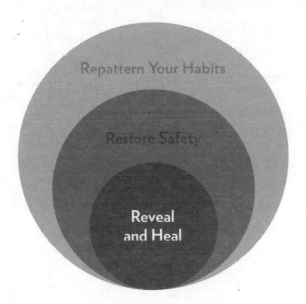

One day when our grown daughters were still young, my friend Julie reached into her rainbow-colored diaper bag and pulled out a book. "I'm reading this," she said. It was *The Descent of the Child*, by Elaine Morgan. In it, Morgan poses an interesting question: Does the adult produce the child or does the child produce the adult?

We tend to look at babies as moving toward adulthood, as if the adult life is the pinnacle of our life journey. What if, though, we could look toward babies and children to remind ourselves of our true nature—freely self-expressive, unself-conscious, uninhibited, and free of the rules that bind us.

In Part 1 of the Inner Freedom Framework, we reveal those experiences that wore away this freedom, when you decided it was safer to hide. And we aim to "make right" those experiences, so you feel restored to your sense of wholeness and open self-expression, as you had as a child.

2

See Yourself Succeed

*"If you change the way you look at things,
the things you look at change."*
WAYNE DYER

OPENED MY INBOX to find an email from Lena. "I have a presentation next week that I'm freaked out about," she'd written. "I know I have to address my fear in a deeper way, but is there something I can do right now?"

Maybe you, too, know that your speaking anxiety deserves some focused attention, but you have something coming up that you urgently need to survive, and you're looking for a quick solution. I have one for you: mental rehearsal, or visualization. In it, you imagine creating the outcome you most desire.

Perhaps you've heard that Olympic athletes use mental rehearsal as part of their practice routine. Swimmer Michael Phelps famously used the technique before he won a gold medal and broke the world record in spite of his goggles springing a leak so he couldn't see. As part of his practice, he had visualized various worst-case scenarios, such as water blurring his vision. Then when it happened, as it sometimes did, he wasn't fazed.

It's not only athletes who use mental rehearsal. Musicians use it too. Decades ago, when I was learning to play Transylvanian village music as a bassist, one of my Hungarian teachers suggested that some of the practice time be spent on imagining playing rather than actually playing. He said that this would accelerate the learning process. Studies back up this idea that you can burn in new patterns into your neurophysiology with visualization. That's why if you are bedbound after surgery, you can keep your muscles from atrophy by visualizing movement.

The human imagination is very powerful. You can harness it to your advantage when it comes to speaking, anywhere and anytime. You invite an image of the desired experience and create the neural pathways to make it happen.

I first utilized mental rehearsal for meetings I dreaded. Maybe you've been part of similar discussions, in your family, with friends or at work—ones strained by complicated group dynamics, grudges, and disagreements. They were *not* something I looked forward to attending, ever. The messy group dynamics were confusing at best, and often frightening.

Out of self-preservation, ahead of these meetings, I would imagine how I wanted to feel (relaxed and at peace). I'd envision myself speaking honestly and seeing the other people being receptive to my words. I'd then spend a moment picturing how I wanted to feel afterward. I'd see us sharing a warm hug or exchanging appreciation and imagine myself feeling content with how it went.

The ones that I mentally prepared for felt significantly better than those I didn't prepare for. In the former, I'd end feeling a sense of satisfaction and connection. In the latter,

I'd leave grumbling under my breath. Perhaps the energy that I visualized and then brought in myself to the group contributed to the overall energy, and that, in turn, served to help us get through the ordeal with more patience and understanding.

Lena practiced this technique every day for a week. She imagined her engaged audience. Their eyes sparkled, and they nodded and smiled as they agreed with the problem that she outlined and the solution she proposed. She saw herself deliver her talk with grace and power, as if the words were coming directly from her soul. She answered questions with authenticity and confidence. A reporter in attendance interviewed her for a news article. Afterward, she envisioned investors giving her their business cards and setting up times to discuss the opportunity.

The following week, Lena emailed me with an update. She said that thanks to that exercise, she had been calmer and more present than she'd ever been in front of a big audience. Neither her hands nor her voice had shaken. She made eye contact with people naturally and smoothly. Even though her fear of speaking was still with her, just as it was for me on Periscope, she was able to control it for the event. Lena felt this was major progress.

I suggest all my clients use this technique daily leading up to a big event. Every time they feel a twinge of anxiety about the gig, I tell them to use that feeling as a reminder to drop into their visualization. They are amazed at how calm and composed they feel when they do. If you practice staying in a place of energetic ease and expansion, you will feel calmer and more composed too.

START WITH THIS

Put yourself in a relaxed state. In hypnosis, this is called "induction." Take time to fully relax your muscles and your breathing, bringing yourself as deeply as you can to what you imagine is your center. That might be in your belly, your heart, a line inside and along your spine, or something else.

Begin to picture the upcoming situation or event as you would ideally like it to happen. See yourself performing the way you would love to see yourself; see other people responding just the way you would love them to feel and respond. Picture yourself at your very best, most effective, powerful, and dynamic.

The more detailed you get, the more you will provide your body with the experience. Imagine handling mishaps with poise and calm or humor. Visualize the outcome, particularly how you feel and how others feel, how you interact with one another. Imagine how you feel when you leave and how you think back on the event.

3

Review to Reveal

*"Our fears are a treasure house of
self-knowledge if we explore them."*
MARILYN FRENCH

LET'S GO ON a little journey in your imagination. Think of a
favorite place in nature. Perhaps it's the seashore or
maybe in the woods. It might be a desert canyon or
on a mountain summit. See yourself from afar, like you're
watching a movie. Notice what you are doing. What do you
see there? What do you hear? Can you feel the wind on your
face, the warmth of the sun, or the coolness of the shadow?
Is there a fragrance in the air?

Next, notice how you feel inside. This is a favorite place,
so I hope you feel good. Really good—alive and free, relaxed
and open and at peace. Pause to savor these good feelings
inside as you look around at the beauty. Notice how you
experience this ease in the presence of the trees, the ocean,
the meadow, the desert, or the stream. Relax into this favorite scene.

Wouldn't it be amazing to have the same presence in front of a crowd as you do in your special spot? To be able to feel freely yourself when you stand in front of the camera lens? To feel articulate, playful, alive?

People work with me because they want to be more comfortable when they present at their workplace, conduct virtual events, speak on a stage, or build their online presence. They want to feel free, more confident, and naturally themselves.

When I ask them what crosses their mind during these times, they share all kinds of worries. "What will people think?" "Do I look awkward?" "I'm afraid I'll mess up." "I'm afraid of being judged." "What if I stumble or forget what I want to say?" "What if I don't know the answer to a question?" "Why would anyone want to listen to me, anyway? I don't have anything special to say."

They also describe what happens to them physically—how they freeze like a deer in the headlights, speak too fast or too softly, how their heart races, their hands sweat and shake, their mouth turns dry, or how their face turns red.

Here's the conflict. On one side, you have the desire to be in that state of presence that's powerful, effective, and fun. And on the other side, you have this other stuff—the stuff in your head, the stuff in your body, in your emotions. And all of this stuff pulls you away from the place of presence you want to be in.

If you want to be in that state of empowered presence you desire, you need to clear the stuff that keeps you from it. Deal with the stuff, and you will be free to delight in the limelight.

Your Psychic Closet

When my daughter, Lexi, turned seventeen, she was inspired to wash her own laundry. I was like, *Hooray!*

After the washer and dryer, she carried her laundry basket back up to her tiny bedroom, turned it over, and dumped the clothes on the floor into a yard-high pile. That pile would stay there like a friend invited over for a one-night sleepover but who stayed a week.

Sure enough, days later, Lexi called out, "Mama! I can't find my spandex!"

I peeked down the hall. She was on her knees next to her pile of clothes, flinging items left and right.

When I looked into her room later that day, only a few items were on the floor. I opened her closet and there was her pile, shoved in! Hmm, now where did she get that idea?

I have to admit: my own closet is packed with stuff on the floor. I've got piles to maybe give away, but not quite yet. There's my basket of yarn waiting to be turned into sweaters, which has gathered dust for a decade. There's a shelf of gorgeous fabric I purchased in Milan in my twenties. I must have been under a spell then. As I rubbed the wool, silk, and brocade between my fingers, visions had appeared of the dresses and jackets I'd make. Nope. Still on the shelf, decades later.

I have a drawer just for junky T-shirts and shorts to wear in the garden. Whenever some well-loved shirt gets stained, I add it to that drawer. I've got stuff in there that I haven't used in several years. Gosh, some of it is thirty years old! I keep it around because I love the design on the fabric, or the fit, or because Dad bought it for me on the only occasion he shopped with me (if you call waiting out on the sidewalk for me to make a decision "shopping with me").

I used to think this behavior was thrifty. Reuse, recycle, and all of that. But the truth is, it's clutter. Even when I ignore it, it affects me on some level. It bothers me. It's a burden, a distraction. And we don't store clutter just in our drawers and closets. There's clutter in our minds as well.

While in grad school for my master's degree in Expressive Therapies and movement studies, I read up on Swiss psychologist Carl Jung and his exploration of the psyche. You might know of Jung from concepts he coined: introversion, extroversion, archetypes, and synchronicity. Jung believed the psyche holds all we've experienced in the conscious and unconscious mind.

I imagine the psyche like a closet. A psychic closet filled with everything that we've ever experienced throughout all the years of our lives: flashes of images and memories, snippets of thoughts and emotions. Some of these past experiences are infused with pleasure, like the time you raced your bike down the neighborhood hill and felt the wind in your hair, or when you swung high on a swing.

Some past experiences we'd rather not remember. They don't feel very good. Like when your fifth-grade teacher called you to the board to point to Romania and you had no idea where it was and started to cry. Or the shame when you were picked last for the soccer game. Even though you hated soccer!

Throughout the years, we accumulate more and more stuff. Every day, new experiences, successes, and challenges are added to the psyche. These experiences can affect us for a long time after they happen, even without our realizing it.

I read a study from Hope College about participants who were asked to think back on a time when they felt mistreated or offended. The researchers measured dramatic increases in their blood pressure, heart rate, and sweat gland activity.

When the participants ruminated on the occurrences, anger, sadness, and anxiety came back to the surface.

What this means is, memories aren't just disembodied thoughts that float around in our heads. Memories are imprinted in our neurophysiology. They live on in our bodies. They have the power to instantly affect our mood in a real, physical, and emotional way.

My mom was a queen of holding on to stuff, both material and emotional. Whether grievances against her neighbors who hadn't invited her to some party or the sublime memory of the most beautiful performance of the *Sleeping Beauty* ballet performed by a Russian legend, her memories were sharp and clear.

When she had dementia in her later years, although she lost the details of her memories, the emotions they evoked were just as transparent and immediate. On my last visit to her, Mom held a photograph of her college graduating class. "Linda, come here, I want to show you something!" she said. She pointed to an attractive young woman in a smart overcoat and a hat fashionably tilted to one side.

"You see this one?" Mom asked. "What an awful person! I hated her. She thought she was better than everybody." Mom practically spat out her words.

"And you see this one?" Worry lines appeared on her forehead as her finger moved to another young woman whom I knew to be her lifelong friend, Jessica. "I don't know what happened to her. She went somewhere and when she came back, she was sick and died. I don't know why." Her voice trailed off in sadness.

"Now, this one!" Mom's eyebrows shot up with excitement and she shook her shoulders seductively. She was pointing to her younger self. "Now, this one was va-va-voom!"

Even with dementia, Mom's memories lived on, complete with their imprint of physicality and emotion. Our brains are this powerful!

Memory Triggers

I attended a farm dinner event where we were asked to share the best piece of advice we'd been given. The gentleman on my right turned to me and said he was told that if you are going to wash a pot, wash the outside as well as the inside.

Wouldn't you know it: every single time I scrub a pot now, I think of that man, that warm summer night under a tent at that local farm, and yes, I do wash the outside of the pot. This is a cool thing about how our brains work. We associate the things we do on a continuum with past experiences.

As we go about our day, we don't have the patience or interest to rummage through all the collected memories associated with our activities. It would take way too much time. Nearly everything we do in our day—wash dishes, drive a car, tie our shoes—has numerous associations with it. Beneath our conscious awareness, the body, in its brilliance, stores all these accumulated experiences with flashes of images, memories, and emotions. In this way, your past experiences along with their associated feelings fire throughout the day in a subconscious way.

When my daughter Lexi was little, if I said to her, "We're off to the beach today," she'd say "Yay!" without any hesitation. She didn't need to think through what happened the last time she was by the shore. The stored memories sent up immediate associations around the beach that were pleasurable and desirable.

If I said to her at that same time, "We're off to music class," she'd immediately cry "NO! I don't want to go!" with panic in her voice. The fear that arose within her signaled danger. She didn't need to go through the entire memory of being "alone" in some room with strangers for an hour, without mommy nearby. The idea of the beach triggered happiness. The idea of music class triggered fear.

As time passes and we get further away from our experiences, like my mom, we may forget the details, but we still feel the emotional and physical imprints of those experiences.

When I prepared to go on Periscope every day those eleven weeks, I didn't think, *Oh, geez, because my sisters kicked me as a kid, I'm afraid to be on camera.* No. All I was aware of was my pounding heart that shouted, "Danger, danger!" In this same way, the fear you feel when you put yourself out there is just the "visible" part of your experience, the part you can sense. It's like an iceberg that shows a small bit of ice above the water's surface, while its foundation goes deep. There is much more to your stress and anxiety than what appears on the surface.

Fear, when looked at in this way, is a message of something deeper, not just some random emotion without cause, to be pushed through or ignored. But that's what we do with our emotions. We try to get rid of them without looking to see what they want to say.

It's kind of like dandelions.

There is a multimillion-dollar business built up to eliminate dandelions from our lawns. Those who oppose dousing the earth in toxic chemicals may spend hours digging dandelions out by hand. The mindset for both types of gardeners is, "Kill the weeds." Then there are those who suggest, "Eat the weeds!" Dandelion diet, anyone?

When I was a farmer, I came across a different and helpful perspective: Weeds are indicators of what's beneath the surface. For instance, deep-rooted weeds like dandelions are an indication of compacted soils. When the soil is hard and compacted, grass and vegetables have a harder time spreading their roots and getting the nutrients they need. Dandelions do well in those soils because of their long, strong taproot.

You can curse the dandelion and possibly douse your landscape in herbicides, or you can listen to the dandelion's message and solve for that. Loosen up the soil, and voila! Fewer dandelions!

Societally, we treat our uncomfortable emotions like we do our dandelions. We might douse them with chemicals, food, drugs, and alcohol. We might try plowing them over so we don't see or feel them. I suggest we look at stress and anxiety as indicators of deeper causes and solve for them. When looked at in this way, the fear, stress, and anxiety offer us the very pathway that could help us thrive.

If we want to transform our fears, we need to first discover what the heck happened and is still happening through our memory imprints that puts us in a state of anxiety.

When I work with clients, they are often surprised by the emotions that bubble up when they remember certain experiences. They'll say, "Oh, that happened a long time ago. I'm not a child anymore." Or "I thought I had already dealt with that in therapy!" And "I don't know why I still feel emotional about this."

As you now know, just because an occurrence happened long ago, doesn't mean that it doesn't still lurk in the background of your psyche and affect how you respond to situations today.

The Three Types of Psychic Clutter

When I had my "duh" moment on Periscope, at first I thought that past experiences were the extent of the source of my fear, or anyone's fear. But as I worked more with clients, I came to see that there isn't only one type of clutter in the psychic closet that impacts us negatively and keeps us constrained—there are three types:

- **Past experiences:** For example, when you were pressured, ridiculed, shamed, rejected, threatened, or hurt.

- **Beliefs:** Beliefs that you came up with in conclusion to your experiences, or ones that you absorbed from your family, community, or society (more in chapter 4).

- **Negative thoughts:** The constant barrage of negativity you serve up for yourself. It's remarkable what we tolerate from ourselves that we wouldn't from another person (more in chapters 5 and 6).

Your fear isn't one big lump of "I'm afraid to speak" or "I don't do well on camera." When you don't feel safe in the limelight, it's not because of one past experience, one belief, or one negative thought. No. It's a whole conglomeration of stuff, and as you go through life, more and more stuff gloms onto the first stuff. I call this "agglutination."

That's why fear feels so complicated and crushing. When you step into the limelight, all of these triggers fire off at once. This is why I find it useful to tease the elements apart, so you can see them more clearly. In order to move forward and thrive, you need to detangle and declutter all this stuff that keeps you from your full, authentic presence.

The Gift and Opportunity of Fear

While it can seem like a lot of work to dredge up old memories, it's actually a gift in disguise. If you just go about your familiar day to day, you remain innocently unaware of the limiting beliefs and clutter you drag around with you. They feel so familiar by now that you hardly notice them, and you have found resources to work around them.

Whether or not you deal with them, these experiences will still operate in the background of your mind and body. They take up precious mental bandwidth and memory, just like apps that run in the background of a computer. They suck your energy and life force. They impact the choices you make and what you see as possible or within your reach. They prevent you from feeling fully you, relaxed, engaged, and in the zone.

Once you uncover and review the stuff of your psychic closet, though, you have the opportunity to resolve and heal all this stuff that keeps you from loving the limelight.

START WITH THIS

You can start your journey with this prayer and intention, or create one of your own:

May I be open to the process of transformation before me.
May I discover the wounds of the past and put them to rest.
May I step into a new day with confidence and ease as I speak.
May this journey carry me forward toward the fulfillment of my desires and dreams.

4

Look Inside Your Closet

"If you're going to clean the house,
you have to see the dirt."
LOUISE HAY

WISH THAT EVERYONE could grow up in an environment that nourishes them, where they feel safe and free to express themselves. Heck, I wish I'd had that. But let's get real. It wasn't that way for many of us. We have far to go to create family, education, work, community, and social media environments that foster self-esteem, emotional safety, and conscious communication. And even in the best ones, there can be inadvertent trauma or harm.

Luckily, you don't need to have had a perfect environment in order to get over your fears of being seen. You just have to address it in a meaningful, effective way. And in fact, when you take this journey and come to the light and freedom on the other side, the sense of ease and confidence will taste that much sweeter.

In this chapter, you'll take inventory of your psychic closet. The psychic closet is different from a real closet in that not all of the contents are equally visible at a given time. Start with what emerges first. What you encounter and resolve will significantly and positively change your experience for the better. Later, new awareness will arise. That's fine and to be expected. It will be icing on the cake, a rewarding refinement that continues to unfold over time.

Resistance

Before we get into it, I want to acknowledge that for some of us, looking at our vulnerable areas can feel uncomfortable. Even when we are alone with ourselves, we tend to move away from what feels bad.

Let yourself be where you are. You may have been taught not to show pain; you may have been ignored, dismissed, or even blamed when you got hurt. Or in contrast, your parents may have paid attention only to the drama and otherwise you felt ignored.

I suggest you remove the judgment and pull out those magic pebbles of understanding and compassion. When you go into your psychic closet and begin to review your past experiences, emotions may arise: shame, anger, sadness. Even "mini traumas" carry a weight for your younger self.

It's not bad or wrong to have experiences in the past that were less than ideal. It's unfortunate, but it's what it is. You are not alone. You are not bad. You are not hopeless.

Emotions are not bad, either. They are designed to help us navigate through life. Difficult emotions that arise when you're looking into your past are simply a confirmation that, indeed, this stuff is still with you and hanging around.

Rather than judge your experiences, invite a sense of curiosity and a stance of observation. Give space for the emotions. Let them move through you. In the next chapter, I will give you tools to help you mitigate and resolve what you uncover.

That said, if you feel fearful that looking at your past will be too much for you to handle on your own, take responsibility and get some outside help. Promise me and yourself that you'll do that.

I have seen that the fastest way to the other side is through. So, take a deep breath and let's dive in.

This Won't Take Forever

If you remember, when I got sick and tired of my daily Periscope "heart attack," made a list of all the healing modalities that I had collected over the years, and was ready to have at it, an invisible arm reached out and put a hand on my shoulder.

No, wait. Before you get rid of it, let's have a look at what that fear actually is.

I closed my eyes to look inside my body. What did the fear feel like? What was it trying to say?

You can try this too. Close your eyes and think of the fear you have of putting yourself out there. See if you can feel where the fear lives in your body. If the fear or stress could talk, what would it say? If something comes up, pull out your journal and write it down. This is a particularly important chapter through which to keep your journal handy or take time to contemplate.

You may be tempted to discount what arises: "It's so minor, it probably doesn't count or matter." Don't do that. A single sentence that has stuck in your memory can make an impact for better and for worse.

It may also be that so many memories come up that you can't possibly imagine sorting through it all. If that's you, take heart from my client Maria. When we began the review process to uncover what past experiences might be the cause of her fear, Maria groaned and said, "OMG, Linda, do we have to go through every story of my life? I don't want to do a therapy thing!"

To her huge relief, we looked at only two or three stories. This intrigued Maria because other, important events had occurred in her life, but just these few stories were enough to unlock the prison.

You don't have to go through every single piece of clutter in order to make an appreciable change in your experience of public speaking. Though, just as when you feel the lightness that comes from a good spring cleaning, you may feel motivated to do more. Because when it's cleared out—wow, so much spaciousness! You feel renewed and energized.

I sometimes get asked if what I do is talk therapy. Yes, we do talk, but while the process of healing I lead you through is therapeutic, it's not "therapy." Yes, it is important to gather enough information to understand what the clutter is about. But you don't have to dwell on it for months or years. Once you've got the ingredients of the issue, it's time to address it and clear it away. But first, let's look at what you have in that psychic closet of yours.

Inventory of Your Past

"Write about a time when you spoke up and it wasn't received the way you wanted."

When I work in groups, I utilize a method called Gateless Writing to uncover stories from the past. Suzanne Kingsbury created this process to quiet the critical mind and connect with your creative source. This creative approach makes the decluttering more interesting and enticing, and helps you access experiences that may not be in the forefront of your mind. You'll hear more about the Gateless process throughout the book.

In this chapter, I'll offer examples to trigger your memories. We'll look at places where we spent the majority of our early life and what might have made us believe we weren't safe: safe at home, safe at school, safe with our peers, and safe in the community. We'll look at the messages we've received about what is and isn't okay in the way we express ourselves; ways that we've felt pressured to conform; experiences and beliefs that may contribute to worry, anxiety, and inhibition.

The first memories to come up may be recent ones. Maybe even now you feel judged at work or in your friend circle or family. Note these in your journal.

Some clients report that they used to feel highly competent and confident about speaking in front of people when they were young, only to have their confidence derailed by a move to a new country or a boss who was highly critical. It may be that this is the single experience you need to clear. However, while you're here, take the opportunity to look around in your past to see what else may have contributed to your fear.

Aim to uncover your earliest memories. Get as close to the root of your fear as you can. The experiences we have in childhood set the foundation for our experiences later in life. Current challenges will often take care of themselves once the earlier experience is resolved.

You may feel you have grown and evolved since these earlier times. You have. But the past can live on in our body's memory, remember? Don't discount the power they may still have on you.

Limiting Beliefs

What makes past experiences so powerful is that we ascribe meaning to our experiences. That means we come to conclusions. These conclusions become embedded as beliefs.

I didn't get that answer right, so I must be stupid.

Dad listens to what my brothers have to say, but not to me, so my ideas must not be important.

Those kids ignored me when I said hello. That means I'm a nobody.

A few years ago, I read *The Big Leap* by Gay Hendricks. He suggests that we have a set point of what we allow ourselves to do. We set an upper limit that keeps us in a particular zone, and every time we stretch ourselves outside of what is familiar and comfortable, we find a way to come back to our set point by sabotage, drama, or illness.

As an executive coach, Hendricks narrowed the beliefs he heard from his clients into the following categories.

* I'm not good enough
* I'm a burden
* It's not safe to outshine
* I don't want to be disloyal

I pondered and journaled about each of these beliefs to see which applied to me. I found, yes, I could definitely relate to the belief that I was not good enough, that I was flawed in some way. Otherwise, I would have had a better work life; I'd have success. Since I haven't had these things, I reasoned, there must be something wrong with me.

It was definitely not okay to outshine my sisters. Later on, it was not okay to outshine friends.

Neither did I want to seem disloyal if I made different choices.

But the belief "I'm a burden" escaped me for a long time. Remember when I said that some stuff in the closet will get revealed at a later time? That's the case here. I had an inkling that this limiting belief played a role in my fear, but for the life of me, I couldn't see it clearly. Delivering produce to a restaurant finally brought me an epiphany.

When I was running a small organic farm growing specialty vegetables for several local restaurants, I especially looked forward to delivery day at two of the restaurants. The chefs would stop what they were doing to chat with me or show off the special pesto with toasted hazelnuts and lemon rind they had created with my mint. Try it out. It's delicious!

Then there was restaurant number three. On my drive over, my heart raced. Week after week for two years, until one day, as my heart raced in its usual way, I tried to investigate what was different about this delivery from the others.

The kitchen was super-small yet high end. As I passed the open prep area, the sous-chefs lit up with smiles.

"Yay, Linda's here!"

In contrast, the head chef was focused on the counter and rarely took time to look up or say hi. I did my best not to bother or bump as I squeezed behind her to the storage area with my enormous cooler. The atmosphere was tense, as if they were running a marathon. In some sense, they were. The elaborate meals had to be ready by the time the diners arrived at five thirty.

This day, I was running late and arrived at five. Even though my produce wasn't needed for that evening's meal, it was not ideal to enter the last-minute frenzy. The chef turned to me and said, "Please don't ever come this late again."

I felt as if I had burdened the busy kitchen in a real way. In that moment, I realized what my racing heart was about. I had felt like a burden to this chef. Not just on this particular day but on most delivery days.

I also realized that it wasn't the first time I had felt like a burden. I felt that way when I was young too. Mom was always vocal about how nice it would be for her when we three girls went away for the eight weeks of summer camp. After camp, back at home, she would say how she looked forward to the start of school so she could have time to herself.

What did I conclude from this? We were a bother and a burden. And that worry of "I'm a burden" fired off on every delivery to that restaurant.

How this experience translates when you speak: "I don't want to take up people's time, so I'll speak fast or not at all."

These four limiting categories of beliefs are useful to understand the ways you, too, might limit yourself. But I have found that there are many more beliefs in our psychic closet, and it's useful, if not vital, to be specific and nuanced rather than try to fit your story and circumstance into a predetermined formula.

Inherited Beliefs

Some of our beliefs don't originate so much from our experiences as much as we absorb them from the surrounding culture.

If you were born in Denmark, the Netherlands, or Japan, you know that it's frowned upon to stand out. The national value is one of equality, so people look to blend in. If you then move to the United States, you'll have to step beyond belief in order to allow yourself to take center stage.

You might have gotten messages from parents or teachers, but it's just as likely that you got ideas from books you read, TV shows, or the media.

"Children should be seen and not heard."

"Boys shouldn't cry."

"Don't contradict your elders."

"Keep your opinions to yourself."

"Don't brag."

My client Karen was brought up in a strict Catholic family. She loved to dance, but anytime she'd twirl around the house, her mother scolded, "Don't be immodest. Don't command all the attention."

Not surprisingly, it's been a struggle for Karen to take center stage. In her career, she purposefully avoided roles and work that might involve public speaking. When the computer company she worked for merged with another, it was recommended that she join the integration group that would be tapped for leadership roles. Even though she knew it was a fantastic opportunity, she found an excuse not to do it.

The problem with both cultural and limiting beliefs is that they hit up against your dreams and desires and your efforts to put yourself out there. For example:

- If you hold the belief that it's not good to stand out, you may resist being a standout onstage.

- If you hold a belief that says you should keep your opinions to yourself, you may hold back your ideas at meetings or avoid the opportunity to lead a team.

- If you believe that authority figures should not be questioned, you may struggle to pitch for a raise or financial investment.

As you take inventory of your own psychic closet, think not just of what happened to you, but also of what you witnessed. As we grow up, our powers of observation teach and inspire us, for better and for worse. I was the goody-goody in my family because I witnessed my sisters get punished when they didn't follow instructions. I watched when Mom washed their mouths out with soap, when she yelled at them and hit them. I have a clear memory of saying to myself, *I'll never do anything to make Mom do that to me.* The irony was that, though Mom never yelled at me, the punishment came around to me via my sisters in their jealousy.

Traumatic Performances

The first and most obvious place to investigate is whether you have ever performed, either onstage or in front of the class or even at home, where you felt publicly humiliated. Maybe you didn't feel prepared. Or you thought you were ready and it turned out you weren't. Or you simply messed up. Or maybe you did great but got criticized.

Maria is a talented writer and editor for a global company. She reached out for help with her terror about an upcoming webinar training five weeks away.

For years, whenever her boss asked her to do a webinar training for their overseas writing department at work, she ran the other way. Her terror of the camera was huge.

But when he asked this time, she thought, *Dang this! I'm not going to die like this. I'm not. I'm going to take this on.*

Maria is someone you'd feel comfortable with. She's thoughtful, shows interest in who you are, and exudes warmth. But speaking to more than two or three people at a time triggered fear. She was afraid she would stumble over her words and say the wrong things, even when she knew the content inside out. She assumed that people wouldn't want to listen to her.

One memory was obvious to her. Because of her natural singing talent, she attended a music conservatory as a teenager, and one day she was chosen to go up onstage to work with a renowned vocal coach during a master class. As she recalled it, this coach shredded her performance phrase by phrase, and the ordeal dragged out for a half-hour in front of two hundred people. She was mortified, ashamed, and, for the first time, afraid to sing. Midway through her next recital, she froze and couldn't find her way back into the song. She walked off the stage and never went back.

This experience devastated Maria. Imagine, also, how you would have felt as a student in the audience to witness someone with a lovely voice torn apart. Do you think you'd be eager to be the next in line?

What did Maria (and likely the students in the audience) conclude? *I'm going to be judged and it's not safe.*

Pressure to Perform

Did your parents have high expectations of you? Did they pressure you to perform well in school? Did you feel like the only time you were really valued was when you were exceptional?

I brought my seventh-grade school report card home and handed it to my mom with a grin.

Mom's reply? "Why an A-minus and not an A-plus?" Grrr!

I've had numerous clients tell me the same story. Some were more terrified of their parents than their teachers.

Amy told me, "The few times I got a bad grade, my parents said I let them down and were heartbroken. What had they done wrong? They took it as a personal attack. I had to succeed in school in order for them to feel okay." The only times Amy felt good enough was when she was exceptional. She pushed to win awards in order to gain her parents' approval, which lasted only briefly before her parents returned to bemoaning their fate.

When clients come to me with imposter syndrome, feeling that no matter how many degrees they have, they are never good enough, this un-please-able parental pattern seems to be a common theme.

You may have felt pressure from parents in other ways. Your parents may have had expectations of how you should act, dress, behave, and even think, and for you, it felt like a straitjacket.

Kathy said, "Mom wanted us to be cookie-cutter images of her. She wanted us to look like her, dress like her, believe the same things. There was no room for different. And I was different." This created in Kathy that not-good-enough self-belief, which kicked in whenever she had to speak to a group.

Ridicule

Connor loved his school in the early years. He felt at home and outspoken and would hang out with his teacher, who felt like his friend. That all changed when his parents sent him to a conservative and competitive boarding school. The teachers and his peers scorned him for his mistakes and wrong answers. Classes were formal and structured, and the students even sat in alphabetical order.

His French teacher read questions out of the textbook one by one to the students in this alphabetical order. Connor could figure out ahead of time which question was his. If he knew the answer, he sighed with relief. But if he determined he didn't know the answer, he'd squirm in anticipation of scorn. Years later, whenever he had to wait his turn to speak, such as when everyone introduces themselves at a workshop, this same anxiety surfaced.

Feeling Ignored, Invalidated, or Invisible

Your thoughts and interests may not have been welcome or respected. Or maybe you simply didn't get the attention you needed. Like Audrey, who told me, "Nothing I did or wanted was ever acknowledged by my parents. They refused to let me study piano, even though I asked year after year. They never came to my school dance recitals. Too much of a bother. No one ever asked me what I wanted or what I thought. Did I needed to be patted on the back? Yes, but they didn't know how to do it. To them it was important to feed me. That was it. Life was just about getting through the day."

As an adult, Audrey picked jobs where she didn't have to share her creativity, thoughts, and opinions. She based most of her job decisions on whether she'd be asked to present at meetings or functions, and turned down jobs because of her fear.

Being Compared to Others

Were you compared to others favorably or unfavorably? Did you hear others compared to you?

Amy felt compared to her mother, and not in a good way. She said, "My mom always showed me pictures of herself as a teen. She was pretty, skinny, and sought-after. I was chubby. I had bad skin and no boyfriends. Mom was a cheerleader and dated all the football players. I felt bad for not being what she wanted me to be."

When you are compared negatively to others, you may conclude you aren't good enough. When others are compared to you and it's uncomfortable, you may feel you have to dim your light so as not to outshine others.

Feeling Like an Outsider

Did your family move a lot? Did you grow up in a different country with a different language? Were your interests, values, or family finances different from those of the cool kids at school? Did you have a different religion, skin color, sexual orientation?

Dev was fifteen when his family moved from India to a small, suburban, mostly white town in the United States. Although he grew up speaking English in addition to his native language, his accent was so different that the kids and his teacher had a hard time understanding him and often asked him to repeat what he said. The kids weren't mean, per se, but they left him alone. Dev focused on his written academic work to get by in school. Although his accent has become more "American" over the years, when he presents at work, he worries about being liked and accepted.

The warm surround of community can make us feel at home, or feel the lack of home and alone. If you felt like an outsider, standing "apart" from the group, as you do when you present to others, your past experiences can magnify these feelings of difference.

Feeling Emotionally or Physically Attacked

Abuse can occur anywhere in our lives from our parents, siblings, teachers, school bullies, or peers. Were you ever criticized, blamed for mistakes you made or problems you struggled with? Were you ever bullied? Did you ever join the bullies?

Maybe you grew up in a family who believed in punishment. Punishments are meant to inhibit your behavior. They are intended to instill fear. It's not surprising, then, that a consequence of physical punishment could be the fear that you'll be attacked if you speak up.

Maria's family held weekly family meetings for her and her five rambunctious brothers to go over plans for the clan and lay down the rules. The meetings began with this recitation:

"Family meeting has begun
No more laughing, no more fun
If you show your teeth or tongue
You will pay a forfeit."

When her brothers giggled and shoved each other, she saw them get punished and was terrified. What did she learn? *As long as I'm quiet, I'm safe. If I speak, I'm in trouble.*

Perhaps it's also obvious that unwanted sexual attention and abuse can impact your sense of safety. Particularly if it comes from within the family, who is supposed to be there to protect and nurture you, or if you felt you had to keep silent, or if you weren't believed. If you feel triggered reading this here, it may be useful to seek professional help to heal this part of your past. If you've already done work on this and it feels manageable, there is no reason not to address it on your own.

Feeling Shamed

Kathy grew up in a conservative family. She said, "We had to be meticulously dressed, show ourselves to be such nice girls, the perfect family. It was all a facade." Kathy felt obligated to hide the "dirty laundry."

At home, the energy was tumultuous. Her mom constantly criticized Kathy, saying, "How can you dress that way? You look terrible. You look like a hussy! Who would ever want you?" When Kathy got bullied at school, her mother's response was, "What did you do to deserve it?"

Although Kathy rebelled against her mother, the feeling of shame and not living up to her mother's standards kept her in behind-the-scenes positions even though she knew she had the potential to take on more leadership roles.

Feeling Judged

If you hear your friends or family pronounce judgments, call others stupid, or look down on people because they have more or less than you, or are in some way different, you may get drawn into the same behavior. This criticism creates insecurity. As you judge others, you would naturally expect the same judgmental view from them. It's like when you hear people gossip behind others' backs. You understand that they can easily do the same to you when you are not around.

Kathy said, "For a long time, I had this belief that everyone who [went] to our [Catholic] church was better than the [people who went to the] Methodist church. They were like the sinners. It was a superiority thing. I still have this in me from my family. I judge when I feel inferior. I judge those who might be judging me."

Not surprisingly, Kathy was convinced of being judged harshly anytime she got up in front of a group.

Being Labeled

I'm not sure why people are so drawn to labeling. Maybe it makes us feel like the world is more understandable and predictable. Many parents will organize their kids like files in a cabinet. "Kyle is the smart one in the family; he comes home with the grades. Max is the artist. Not great with grades, but he loves to draw. We don't know how he'll make a living with that. Cindy is the athlete. She can't sit still to do her homework. All Eddie does is play video games. We don't know what will become of him!"

There's nothing wrong with recognizing a child's strengths and inclinations. The problem arises when this declaration has a value placed on it, or when it becomes a box that you can't climb out of, or when you don't feel seen for who you are because that label is already taken.

My mom always introduced my sister Judith as the dancer in the family. Every time I heard her say that, I wanted to call out, "But I'm a dancer too!" I felt unseen. Maybe you did too.

Competing for Attention or Absence of Attention

Did you come from a big family, fight for airtime, or feel lost in the fray? Connor's father was a gifted teacher and enthusiastic storyteller who was gone most of the time, except for at dinner. From his place at the head of the table, Connor's dad held forth and dominated the airtime. The kids' role was to sit and listen. When his dad took a break, his mom took over. The kids never said anything. Anytime Connor tried to interject a thought, he felt forced back into silence. He was led to believe that what he said didn't matter.

Experiencing Crises, Illness, or Special Circumstances, and Having to Adopt Responsibility

How stable or unstable was your family structure? Did a parent ever fall ill, disappear, or pass away when you were young? Did someone in the family deal with drug or alcohol addiction? Did a sibling have special needs? Or did you have to be the grown-up before you were one?

Amy's dad suffered from depression and she felt it was her job to try to make him feel better. She had to be the parent for her parents. She felt responsible for keeping the family glued together. She never asked for help with her problems. She never asserted her own ideas. She didn't want to overwhelm them any more than they were. She told me, "I cried myself to sleep every night."

After a lifetime of supporting others, when it came time for Amy to promote her business, to put herself front and center, there was an invisible wall. Who was she to be the center of attention? She felt like she didn't have the right to take up space for herself.

Having Vocal Constraints

Sometimes the way into the psychic closet is through our actual voice and how we feel about the sound of it, how it helps us, and how we feel let down by it.

As kids we all get some kind of feedback about our voices and the way we express ourselves. Adults wrangle kids to behave according to what they, the adults, are comfortable with. Were you told you were too noisy, too nosy, too talkative, too shy or quiet? Were you told you were overly dramatic or emotional or intense? Have you received comments even as an adult that your voice isn't up to par in some way?

Lina's family members all have beautiful rounded British accents from their life in Botswana. When she moved to Vancouver as a kid, her accent was erased. She said, "No one in my family could understand me. They would tell me, 'You're mumbling, you don't know how to enunciate, you're swallowing your words.'" Lina became self-conscious when she spoke and self-critical of the sound of her voice, which sounded harsh in contrast to the melodious sounds of her family. This assessment from them and then from herself made her cringe in the limelight.

School Experiences

We already touched on the "performance" activities of school, like when you stood up in front of a class. You may have had a mean teacher and been shamed or bullied and excluded by kids. These experiences will directly impact how safe you feel standing among colleagues or higher-ups in the ranks. But it's not just the negative memories in school that can impact our confidence when we put ourselves out there. The very nature of the structures and values promoted in the classroom can clash with what is needed to speak with confidence in different situations.

I bring this up because I've had a number of clients who felt nurtured at home and did well in school and were perplexed about their stage fright. Upon closer investigation, we discovered downsides and inadvertent consequences of school culture. Have a look and see if any of these resonate with you.

Fear of making mistakes or not knowing the answers In school, we get the highest grades for the fewest mistakes.

To be fair, certain career paths thrive on the absence of mistakes, like accounting, inventory, and such. Unfortunately, the fear of mistakes can paralyze you and keep you from taking risks, trying new things, or allowing yourself to learn something from scratch. It can keep you in places where you feel familiar and a sense of control. This happens to the best of students as well as those who struggle. I've had clients who will keep themselves in their sphere of competence, where they know they will be at their best, rather than risk making a mistake by taking the leap and going after a keynote or going live on social media.

Others are petrified that someone in the audience will ask them questions they don't know the answer to. It's actually not a big deal to not know answers in the real world. But it was in school (more on this in chapter 9).

When it comes to communication, there is no right way to talk about a topic. Although there are "plug and play" elements you can use in your communications, by and large, speaking is a creative expression and requires a hefty amount of "try and see." In school, they may give lip service to "effort," but that is different from encouragement to explore your expression without the fear of the mark you will receive.

Needing to know the full roadmap before you move forward After I made a Facebook post about the hazards of schooling, a successful coach contacted me to describe how in school, she had learned to research first rather than just try something out and see if it worked. She couldn't tolerate the possibility that it wouldn't be perfect, wouldn't be good enough, or wouldn't work at all. This need for thorough and lengthy research impacted how quickly she was able to grow her business.

It reminds me of how you might approach a piece of furniture that you have to put together. My husband *never* looks at the instructions first. It's fun for him to try to figure out by doing. Only if he gets completely stuck will he take a peek at the manual.

Me? Just the opposite. I have to carve out plenty of time. I'll read the instructions before I look through the box. Then I'll read them again as I unpack the parts. Then read them multiple times as I move along. I like the reassurance that I'm doing it the "right way." Yes, I got As in school. How do you think I did it?

Getting graded for following directions My friend's son had problems in third grade. The teacher wanted him to write his name on the upper left side of the paper. He would write his on the right or in the side column or at the bottom of the paper. The teacher thought he was insubordinate and would punish him with low grades. He lost his confidence as a learner all because there was a mismatch of values in the classroom between teacher and student. He failed the class because he failed to understand the point of it all.

This boy is now a tattoo and graffiti artist invited to different countries for his installations. It was a long, hard road for him to claim his expression. I can't help but wonder how his life might have unfolded if his creative paper signature had been valued and enjoyed by his teacher rather than criticized.

Becoming hooked on external validation For those of us who didn't rebel but played the game, schooling may have got us hooked on external validation. We looked to the teacher or someone outside ourselves to tell us we were good enough. We learned to derive our self-worth from external sources rather than from within.

I excelled at figuring out what the teacher wanted and being easy to manage, and so I got good grades. Please the teacher, follow directions, get the reward. My essays in school followed the run-of-the-mill style of opening paragraph, supporting evidence, and summary.

When my college English professor handed me a C grade on my first paper, I was shocked. I had followed the directions and given him what I thought he wanted. It had always "worked." I had never, ever, gotten a C.

What stunned me more than the grade was his reason. He said, "I don't want you to write what you think I want to hear. I want you to write what you think."

What? He didn't want me to write what he wanted? What were these new rules? I didn't get it. What *I* wanted to write about? *My* ideas? Did I have my own ideas?

I honestly didn't have any clue what it meant to have my own ideas. Aside from my shame and anger at him for switching the rules on me, his grade made me curious and set me on a path. It's taken me many years to release the allure of the good-girl role that pleases others. I suspect I'm still in process with it.

When you are caught up in external validation, it makes it hard to trust your own decisions, your own opinions, to take a stance on your ideas and beliefs in front of an audience.

Dampened self-expression A classroom needs order. Learning to manage all the energy among twenty or thirty kids is a real feat, and many teachers struggle with it. Ask any teacher. And as a kid, if you have a wonderful sense of humor, a bit of a prankster in you, and also display leadership skills, where will that land you? Most likely in the principal's office. Often. Yet whom do we love to listen to onstage?

That very same type of person! As a classmate, there is a powerful message sent to you. I know what mine was. Be cooperative; be quiet; be nice to the teacher, and I'll get my grade. Don't stand out. Don't express yourself. It will get you in trouble.

Hampered comprehension Did you ever feel completely overwhelmed by the amount of homework you had? Felt there wasn't time to read a whole book before you had to write a book report? School overloads you with too much material. You're graded for speed and volume. There is no space for deep thought. It just isn't valued as much as covering a lot of territory.

I believe this gets in the way of connecting with ourselves and the material. We don't learn to take the time to think critically and form personal opinions about the world. This is the opposite of what it takes to become truly knowledgeable in an area where you can share your expertise.

Ironically, many kids will say that they didn't learn much in school and they don't feel they have expertise. This self-assessment is unfortunate; it keeps kids hooked on the idea that they have to learn more and more. This affects a person's self-esteem and the sense of value they bring to the world.

Unseen special gifts Granted, other people's responses help us learn to get along, help us grow. But when we are on the school program, our strengths and attributes can be disregarded because they don't overlap with the needs of the classroom and education environment. You might excel with art, music, dance, or design. But unless you are in a school that has the budget for these "extras," you're out of luck.

You might be highly empathic, able to share your vulnerability, a deep thinker, a connector, an experimenter—all skills that can be capitalized on as an adult, but are unrecognized as skills in school. When you grow up, you might understand how these things help you as a speaker or professional networker or a manager, but you still feel unseen.

Treasures to Keep

As you read, you may wonder what to do with all of these memories and feelings you've uncovered. You may be feeling emotional. That's okay. The reason this stuff has stayed buried is that it doesn't feel good.

I want you to pause for a moment. Take a breath and give yourself appreciation for your willingness to go through some emotional upheaval in the service of a greater transformation of your life. I won't leave you in this uncomfortable place for long, I promise. We'll get to clear the causes of discomfort and start healing in the next chapter.

If you've made a master list of all the "unpleasantries" of the past, it's likely you feel relieved to know that there are indeed reasons you're not comfortable being seen and heard. That there is a connection between feeling shut down when you tried to express yourself as a kid and feeling afraid to express yourself now as an adult. That you are not crazy for the feelings you have. That it all makes sense. And that feels good already.

When I look back over my life, I can now connect the dots and see that I've been on a journey to overcome self-consciousness and inhibition, to feel more freely myself, to overcome the feeling of not being safe to be seen, to find my voice and stand by my opinions without apology.

How can you look back and connect the dots in your life? What do you do now, or can you imagine doing, in spite of or because of the experiences you've had? What strengths do you have because your parents demanded perfection if you were to be worthy of their praise and you got it only on report card days of straight As? And on every other day of the year, you were otherwise unseen. Did you develop an amazing work ethic? Persistence?

Greta had a successful, angry, and overbearing father. At work, she entered into a male-dominated field. On the one hand, she suffered from the messages she received from men about her self-worth. On the other, after reclaiming her worthiness for herself, she realized that she possessed a superpower from this difficult relationship with her father— an ability to handle difficult people and tense environments.

What resourcefulness did you develop in yourself because you were bullied as a kid? Did you develop an ability for introspection or empathy for those who sit on the sidelines? Did you learn how to set limits and stand up for yourself or trust your intuition? Maybe you're on a mission to help others in some way because of the experience you had. These are some of your gifts born of surviving the little and big traumas of your upbringing. These are the keepers, the treasures in your psychic closet.

We humans thrive on growth and transformation. The process itself is empowering. You just may find that because of the negative experiences you had, you now possess some special power that can positively impact the world. Keep an eye out for these treasures.

START WITH THIS

Open a page in your journal or ponder. What memories came to you as you read through this chapter? Allow yourself some time to explore them in your writing. If you prefer, find a buddy to share this process with, or start a group.

5

Heal What You Reveal

---

*"Getting over a painful experience is a lot like
crossing monkey bars. You have to let go at some point
in order to move forward."*

C. S. LEWIS

A ZEN PARABLE TELLS us of an old monk and a young monk who were traveling through the forest when they came to a rushing river. There on the bank stood a young woman with a basket of goods. She turned and asked if they would carry her across the river. The two monks looked at one another. It was forbidden for them to touch a woman.

Then, without a word, the older monk bent down and allowed the woman to get on his back. He carried her across the river, put her down, and the two monks continued on their way.

The old monk walked peacefully, but not the younger monk. He became more and more agitated with every mile. Finally, he could hold back no longer and blurted out, "How could you have carried that woman on your back? You know it's forbidden!"

The old monk calmly replied, "I put the woman down on the other side of the river. Why are you still carrying her?"

How nice it would be to be like the older monk—able to let go of past experiences in an instant! First off, you have to want to. Not everybody does. Take my mom.

I grew up on Long Island in New York, and Mom loved to drive into the city for the latest exhibit at the Guggenheim or an off-Broadway matinee. The city is notorious for its crazy drivers. Mom prided herself in being one of them. You could expect that an even more aggressive driver would cut in from the right side in a near miss. Mom would yell every Yiddish curse she knew at him (it almost always was a "him"). "Schmuck! Schmendrick!"

As a kid I was terrified, but later on, I'd admonish her: "Let it go, Mom. Let's be thankful we're safe!" It was hard for her. To let go of what she considered inconsiderate and dangerous was not her forte. Quite the opposite. She kept track of all the people who had done her wrong over the years.

One day when Mom was in her eighties and in her dementia, I took her to the pool club to sit in the gorgeous August shade. As I looked around at the lounge chairs, I saw a familiar face.

"Oh, look!" I brightened. "There's Mrs. So and So!" I thought Mom would also brighten to see someone to say hi to. Saying hi was one of the niceties at a club.

"Terrible person," Mom said loudly, almost a shout.

"Mom! Don't talk so loud!"

"She's terrible, what she did!"

"What did she do?"

"She had a party and didn't invite me. She's horrible, *horrible*!"

No, Mom was not a letting-go kind of person. She carried that book of crossed-out names until the day she died. It never occurred to her that she could handle bumps in her relationships in any other way.

When you have dreams, it's a whole different game. You're willing to do whatever personal growth it takes to remove the blocks and obstacles that stand in your way. It takes a special kind of person for that, and you are that special kind of person.

In the previous chapter, you uncovered the experiences and messages you received that told you it was unsafe to be seen, heard, or expressively you. Knowing what happened can be an eye-opener. But as the Hope College study indicated, a list of memories won't get you over your fear of speaking.

We carry the stuff of our psychic closet because we don't know what to do with it. If we did, we would have done it already. At the time of these experiences, we didn't have the resources to respond in a way that brought us back to our sense of wholeness. Either our parents or teachers weren't around to help or they were the cause of our distress.

Unresolved past experiences are like landmines that get triggered over and over again. In order for you to move on, the landmine needs to be disabled. You need to unplug the emotional charge from the experience in your memory, so when you recall a situation, you no longer feel the emotion and intensity. It becomes just a memory, not a landmine. You feel back in balance, back to equilibrium, free of the negative self-beliefs that you may have picked up along the way. It's not that these memories disappear. It's more that you let go of the meaning they have for you.

What Is Healing?

When you look to clear the past, there are some things you can change and some you can't. You can't change what happened. No matter how much you go over an incident in your head to change the facts, the facts remain. I don't believe it's helpful to dwell on your stories. Do write about them and use them as teaching points if they are relevant, but then let them go. Most importantly, I want to see you resolve them so that they don't own you, but rather you own your stories and they become just that—stories.

What you can change is how you continue to hold them inside you. You can change what you focus on and your perspective. You can change the meaning you've assigned to your experiences—what they say about who you are and who you aren't, if you are good enough or not, loveable or not, damaged or whole. What it means about what you can and cannot do from now on.

Healing doesn't necessarily happen from a single touch of a specific modality. More often than not, it requires an integrated approach, a weave of several modalities in order to be thorough, effective, and long-lasting.

It's common for this clearing work to bring up tears, so if you're feeling emotional, know that's perfectly normal. You can't really move through something without feeling it. So, let the tears flow. It will pass and you will feel the sweet freedom on the other side.

This might seem like a big project. Yeah, it is. But it's a doable project. And so worthwhile. I was able to clear my fear in five days. I've helped some of my clients get the same results over a long weekend. More typically, we move more gradually over a couple of months. Keep in mind that the short time frames require focus and time free of distraction. Don't get discouraged if it takes you longer. Everyone has their own personal life circumstances and obligations. It's not a race. It will take the time it takes. Honor your process.

I have experimented a lot with what tools to use, what is enough and what isn't enough, to resolve the past and overcome fear and anxiety. Of course, everyone is different.

However, the following five tools are foundational to the clearing process I use with my clients and students: EFT, creative visualization, Gateless Writing, forgiveness, and dance. I'll describe how you can use them for yourself and afterward suggest other resources you may have, plus ways to get creative with your healing.

Emotional Freedom Technique, or Tapping (EFT)

My friend and transformational kinesiologist Eliza Bergeson first introduced me to Emotional Freedom Technique (EFT), or Tapping, in the early nineties. A few years later, I had a dramatic transformation as a result.

I pulled my hair habitually for twenty-five years, ever since I was a teen. With a habit like this, you both love and hate it. I loved the relief it gave me in the moment. But I hated to be enslaved to the habit. I felt I had no choice but to explore my hair with my fingers and pull out strands. This habit created a chronic strain in my neck and shoulders that resulted from holding my hand up to my hair.

When my daughter Lexi was two, she sat directly behind me in the car. Whenever I pulled my hair, which was often, I was acutely aware of her watching me from behind. I didn't want her to emulate me and do what mommy did. I wanted to stop.

I had worked with Eliza earlier on this habit with EFT and it had helped for a while—an exalted seven months. Then I started up again. I tried hypnotherapy. That helped too. I stopped for nine months. But when a big stress came back into my life, my hand crept back up to my hair.

Now, with my daughter's future at stake, I was super-motivated to make a longer lasting change. Every day for the next week, I used EFT, even after I had stopped the habit after day four. I wanted to be good and sure it lasted. And guess what? It has. I haven't pulled my hair for seventeen years!

What I love about EFT is that you don't ignore or push away the problem. You start from where you are. You acknowledge the difficulty of a situation and the feelings around it. As you tap meridian points on your face and upper torso, your body releases its habitual hold on the experience. Somehow the stimulation of the meridians interrupts the default patterns. As the memories are experienced, the body gets to have a new response, a new pattern.

EFT was founded by a fellow named Gary Craig. I was struck by his desire to get this practice out to humanity to help deal with pain, stress, and trauma. The potential is enormous. Numerous controlled studies have shown the effectiveness of EFT in alleviating PTSD with war veterans. If you've tried EFT in the past with mixed results, I encourage you to keep an open mind and give it a go again.

My clients love EFT. In my style, it flows organically and feels like a rinse in the river. It lifts away the burden of your memory and shifts your energy into something new. Lea, who was in a self-study program, wrote me to share her experience of the EFT process. She said, "I wasn't aware of how many thoughts I had lying there in my subconscious. It felt therapeutic to bring them to the surface and acknowledge them. I was a little unsure of how the tapping would make a difference, but I felt so much more aware of the words and their meaning. Each statement was spoken just as clearly as the last, every statement given the recognition it deserved. I did not expect to get emotional, so I was surprised when I did, more than once. And I noticed the statements that shifted me. It was really powerful."

Another student, Siena, said, "I feel lighter, freer, more open, more rooted in myself, more confident. I also feel that it's okay to not be perfect."

Get Started with EFT

Over the twenty-five years that I've used EFT, I've kept some original elements and made some of my own changes. What you see here may be similar to or different from what you've come across elsewhere.

We start off with tapping the edge of the palm of the hand (small intestine meridian in acupuncture) and name the broad issue or circumstance three times. For example:

"Even though my sisters attacked me out of jealousy, I love and accept myself just as I am."

Often, I'll say this first statement a few different ways to cover the experience more broadly—for example: "Even though Mom set me up for my sisters to be jealous of me, I love and accept myself on all levels of being."

Then we move to tapping on particular points of the face and upper chest. We speak bits of words and stories that emerged from the process of taking inventory of your past. And we keep going around and around the points in a circle until we are done with the process. The tapping points are as follows:

Inside edge of eyebrow: *bladder meridian*
Temple (side of eye): *gallbladder meridian*
Under the eye: *stomach meridian*
Under the nose: *governing vessel*
Chin: *conception vessel*
Collarbone knob: *kidney meridian*

Underarm against the ribs: *spleen meridian*
Top of head: *governing vessel*

It's not essential for you to know the names of the meridian points. Just know that as you tap, you innervate eight of the twelve main meridian points in acupuncture.

We start with tapping on the inside edge of the eyebrow. If you and I are doing this together, I say a statement and you repeat it. Then we move on to tapping on the temple. I say another statement, and you repeat it.

When you are doing it by yourself, if you have the space to do so, speak it out loud. If you don't have the privacy, speak silently in your head.

Using my experience with my family, an EFT session might go something like this:

First, I acknowledge what happened and how it felt.

My sisters kicked me
It was scary
It hurt
It felt so unfair
Why did my mother say that?
There was no one to protect me
My sisters hated me
I wanted them to love me
It wasn't safe
It wasn't safe to be me
I couldn't show myself
They called me stupid
They kicked me or held me down on the floor

Now I move into what I would have liked.

I wish it had been different
I wish Mom had been smarter
I wish she had given my sisters attention too
Instead of giving it all to me
I wish we'd all gotten along
All that yelling
All the punishment

Now I bring in self-compassion and understanding of my younger self.

I didn't want to be punished
I tried to be good
I feel bad for that little girl
I loved my sisters
I wanted them to love me too
I wanted them to be happy
To be friends
But that's not how it was

Now I bring in my intention to shift my experience and let go.

I want to let go of this hurt
I want to let go of this fear
This fear of being attacked
It was a long time ago
I'd love to let this all go
To forgive my sisters for their jealousy
For being mad at Mom

I bring in compassion for others, which helps in the letting go process.

Mom was also hurt as a child
She was tied to a tree by her mother
She had her wounds
She didn't have any good models
She didn't know better
If she could have done better, she would have
I forgive her and let it go
I forgive my sisters and let it go
I forgive myself and let it go
I am older now and more capable
I can protect myself now
I can stand up for myself
And set my boundaries

Now I affirm my new state of being.

I am free to express myself now
I am free to say what I want now
I don't need to be afraid of my sisters anymore
I don't need to be afraid of Mom punishing me anymore
It feels good to have this all in the past
And to feel free
Free of the burden
Free of the fear

I end with gratitude and appreciation.

I'm grateful to let this go
I'm grateful for all that I've learned
All that I'm still learning
How I'm becoming more and more me

How I'm more and more able to express my true self
To speak my truth
To be bold
I love and accept myself just as I am.

As you can see, I fold other practices into the EFT: forgiveness, letting go, compassion, gratitude, loving-kindness. I find it useful to incorporate a certain amount of redundancy when clearing. For instance, you'll see more practices for forgiveness below, but weaving it into the EFT helps shift the emotional readiness for letting go.

This script is here for you to use as a beginning template. When you actually do the tapping, allow yourself to follow your intuition and vary from the path.

My client, Corinne, did EFT on her own. This is what she said about the experience.

Although I wrote a script based on Linda's, I made space for more to come up than what I had written, and it took me down a path I didn't anticipate. More examples of things from my past came up and I was able to notice and acknowledge the feelings that were associated with them.

I uncovered anger and some other feelings I didn't know were there. I found it very cathartic, validating, and illuminating. I tapped for at least fifteen minutes, and kept going until I felt a sense of completion and peace at the end. Even if people are skeptical about the energy component of tapping, I find that simply giving my unfiltered thoughts a voice is powerful in itself.

Another client shared that just the process of writing her script was powerful and healing. She said, "I love what came out of it! It helped me reframe some old 'ways of being' and more consciously reclaim my right to self-expression as a sensitive empath!"

To watch an EFT tutorial, and to get all the resources that go with this book, go to delightinthelimelight.com/resources.

Creative Visualization

I first came across the idea of affirmations and creative visualization in Shakti Gawain's 1978 book, *Creative Visualization*. When this book came out, there was nothing else around like it. A how-to book on harnessing our imagination to create what we want in our lives was groundbreaking.

Our imaginations are powerful. We use them to envision what we'd like to do and create. We also imagine bad things— what people might think if you post a video; that no one will applaud after you speak.

As a tool for clearing, we can use our imagination to heal our past. Here are three powerful visualizations you can use:

- Revisit your experience from the past but recreate it in a way that would have felt empowering. Invite a fairy godmother, a secret friend, a device, or a superhero to accompany you to make it turn out in a way that brings you back to wholeness.

- Imagine you are going to cut the cords that bind you to these past experiences. Picture in your mind the people who were involved. What do you need to say to them in order to feel ready to cut the cord and feel like it's over for real?

* In your imagination, visit with your future self, who is beyond your current state of stress and anxiety. Listen to what encouragement and wisdom they offer you from their future perspective.

Recreating an experience the way we would have liked it to happen allows us to feel the possibilities we now actually have available to us that we didn't have before. You might think that this is an empty fantasy—"if only this could have happened, it would have been so nice"—but it's much more. It's taking the reins of your life and creating a new experience for yourself that is filled with what you need and desire.

When you revisit a past experience with a fantasy helper, you bring out your higher wisdom to share from your current, more mature and experienced life. You care for your past self in the way you needed to be cared for, you speak to them in the way they needed to be spoken to at the time. We can't avoid all negative experiences. But we want the resources to handle them in the best way possible. We want them to not hold us back from feeling free and empowered.

Similarly, when visiting our future self, we are able to confirm our trust in ourselves that we will indeed someday be on the other side of the current obstacle that keeps us from showing up naturally ourselves in our life and work. And that within us is counsel to help us navigate our journey forward with grace.

When you prepare to do a visualization, begin first by relaxing your body deeply, in all your cells and tissues, from head to foot. With your mind's eye, travel inside your body to notice where you may be holding tension, and as well as you can, soften it up.

Relaxation puts you in a more open state. In hypnosis, they might say you are more open to suggestion. I would explain it a bit differently. Your objective is to change the neural pathways, the patterning. If you are tense, you are closing off the neural pathways in your body. So by relaxing, before imagining, you are allowing change to happen.

Once you have your nice, relaxed state, begin your chosen visualization. If you are recreating a past experience, start with that experience. Imagine how you would have liked it to play out. You can play it out in different ways.

When I have a visit with my future self, I like to imagine a favorite, special, or magical place for the rendezvous. A mountaintop or field of flowers. First create your place—how it looks, the scent and sounds, your feeling there—and then let your past or future self come into view. Let yourself have an exchange. Offer a hug, a gift, an elixir, or shared drink. Share your words. Look into each other's eyes. When you are finished, say goodbye.

In any of these visualizations, don't worry about doing it "right." It's not important to clearly see in your visualization. I don't have a clear image most of the time. Rather, it might be a flash or just a sensation of the place and person. This is for your benefit and you can do it the way it works for you.

Gateless Writing

According to University of Texas psychologist James W. Pennebaker, a pioneer of writing therapy, journaling can be successfully used to recover from upsetting, stressful, or traumatic life events.

I find it helpful to write through uncomfortable emotions to get a sense of what's going on inside. Somehow, the process of putting words on paper (or in a computer document) can help you work through your feelings better than stewing them in your head.

Here are some ways you can use the writing process for healing:

- Just as with visualization, begin by taking a few minutes to connect with your body. Close your eyes and look inside. Feel into different parts of your body. Notice your breath as it flows in and out.

- Set a timer for three, five, or ten minutes. Pick one of the past experiences you uncovered earlier and allow yourself to write, without edits or forethought, about what you remember. What were your thoughts and feelings? Imagine that you are sharing the story with a friend. What would they ask you about it? Write that down.

- If your past experience included other people, try this practice I call the "Early Life of So and So." When I chose the name, I was inspired by Wikipedia, which in the biography of a person includes a description of their early life that may be relevant to whom they've become. Let's say the "offending person" in your story was a relative, teacher, or another school kid. Write a backstory, as if you were a novelist. Everyone starts out life as an innocent child. What happened to them that created the person they've become? What were their hopes and dreams, and where did they get hurt or stunted? You don't have to write fact. It can be total fiction. When people are hurtful or mean, we tend to think it's because of who we are. It's actually more about who they are. When you create their backstory, it can help you create some distance and compassion for this person.

- Record your experiences from the other healing modalities. What did you discover when you used your creative visualization to come up with a fantasy helper? How did it feel and what did you notice when you did the EFT? When you take the time to note down your experiences, you deepen the integration and increase its meaning. It also serves as a record you can return to in order to see the distance you've covered in your journey.

Forgiveness

"Forgiverance" is a made-up word. I like it because sounds like "forgiveness" and also like "deliverance," which means "to set free." Forgiverance is forgiveness that sets you free.

When I first became aware of the memories from my childhood during my Periscope epiphany, I got to work. I forgave my sisters, and I forgave my mom and dad. I tried to remember everything that happened to me that hurt me or made me feel slighted and let it go. Whatever went on in school, at summer camp, any punishment, scares, the time that girl punched me in the stomach in the stairwell at school, the time that the cool girls in seventh grade decided "no one talk to Linda."

I spent hours in bed at night combing through my past for all of the negatives that had been said or done to me. Then I forgave the players. I didn't know for sure which of my memories affected my speaking confidence, so I went through it all—everything I could remember, even though I might have "dealt" with it before. You never know what lingers on, and I sure didn't want anything to hold me back, conscious or unconscious.

Let me be clear: When I speak about forgiveness, I'm not suggesting that you seek out and interact with a person who did you wrong. Nor is the practice of forgiveness I describe here to be confused with condoning the actions of others. The purpose is to disallow these ghosts of times past to hang on to you, pull you down, or divert your attention from your dreams and desires.

It may seem that by holding on to your anger or resentment, you are punishing the other person. That may have some truth. You may be. But it's also true that the one you hurt most is yourself. To make forgiveness work, you gotta want it. You have to feel like you don't want to carry stuff around anymore. If you don't want to let go, you won't. Mom didn't want to forgive her ex-friends; she held on to her grudges rather than letting go. It kept her trapped in spite of her conviction that she was on the right side of justice.

This is how I look at forgiveness: It's your declaration that you've carried the pain long enough and you're ready to be free and lighten your load. It's your decision to release the emotional hold that some wrongdoing has on you. It's saying that you're not going to define yourself by what happened. You can't change the past, but you sure can change what you carry around with you. We often blame ourselves for either the harm that comes to us or our inability to deal with the situation. When you use forgiveness as an inner practice and a technique to clear the clutter of the psychic closet, you forgive others, the circumstance, and most importantly yourself.

All that said, forgiveness is more easily done with people who are no longer part of your life or in relationships that have already made positive change. It's more difficult to forgive a person who maintains the behavior that you suffered from in the first place—for example, a narcissistic parent who continues to dismiss your accomplishments. It feels impossible to forgive them when the same old stuff is current. In such cases, I recommend the following:

- Do the work here. The reason is, you can't change what other people do, but you can change what you decide it means about you.

- Reduce your exposure to them. Look at how you can redraw your boundaries. If it's your parent, can you call them less? If it's a co-worker, can you create an arrangement so that you communicate in a different manner?

- Create a visualization in which you see yourself playing a different role or responding in a completely different way. A way where you seem to be immune, above, maybe even compassionate. But definitely separate.

- Strategize responses that you can pull from in the moment that will either help you maintain your distance or shift the energy for you.

Forgiveness Practice 1: Letter of Forgiveness
When you have a long list of folks or circumstances to forgive for what seem like minor offenses, it might be tempting to use shortcut statements—"I forgive you, Jack; I forgive you, Jill; I forgive you, Professor Whatever-your-name-is."

Take the process a step deeper by adding specific details. For example, "I forgive you for telling me to not interrupt you"; "I forgive you for not coming to my dance performance."

However, the practice feels even more gratifying and potent when you expand upon your feelings with a perspective of compassion and understanding. After all, wounded people wound others, and everyone does the best they can with the resources and skills they have at the time.

Here's what this process looked like for my client Katie, in the form of a letter:

Mom, I forgive you for not always knowing how to parent me, your child who's a different race from you. You did the best you could. It probably never occurred to you that the world would see me any differently from how you saw me. It was a different time, and the conversations around racial identity and mixed-race identity are different from how they are today. You were busy breaking barriers that most immediately affected you.

I forgive myself for being angry at you and believing that you did not love me. It was a misunderstanding. I forgive myself for assuming the worst in you and not recognizing that you were fighting for me too.

I let go of the expectation that just because you are the parent, you will automatically know better. I let go of the expectation that who I am is defined by what others think. I give myself permission to speak up for myself. I allow myself to stand as I am.

Forgiveness Practice 2: The Four Forgiveness Mantras
I'm sorry. Please forgive me. Thank you. I love you.

When I came across these four mantras in 2015, I was intrigued. The words are so simple, but they felt awkward at the same time. Who was I saying thank you to? Who was I saying I love you to? Did it matter? Were the words magical on their own? Did they have to be spoken in a particular order?

The first line, "I'm sorry," can mean I'm sorry for anything I or my ancestors did intentionally or unintentionally to contribute to this situation. What I love about this is that even if I feel victimized by a situation, I can totally appreciate the interconnectedness of life and karma beyond my personal awareness and understanding. In any case, whatever comes my way or whatever I have knowledge of is mine to deal with.

Bring a situation to mind that calls for forgiveness, either for yourself or for another. Slowly repeat the phrases: *I'm sorry. Please forgive me. I love you. Thank you.*

Don't get hung up on the order. Let whichever phrase comes naturally to you come out. There is no wrong or right here. Don't worry about who you are forgiving or asking forgiveness from, or if when you say "I love you" you direct it toward yourself, another person, or the universe. Simply allow yourself to enter into the states of forgiveness, love, and gratitude.

Dance

Too often we try to solve problems in our heads, with words and language. However, we live in our bodies and experience ourselves in our cells and tissues. It's in our body that our feelings reside. We underutilize the power of movement in our lives. We'll use it for pedestrian purposes, to get where we're going or for fitness, but too rarely to express ourselves and as a mode of healing.

Take a look at cultures around the world, though, and you'll find various ceremonies and shamanistic rituals that incorporate music and dance to maintain and return to health, well-being, and equilibrium. Humans are meaning-making creatures. We've created rituals and found ways to heal for centuries.

In Morocco, the Sufis and Gnawa conduct ceremonies during which they drum, sing, and dance to overcome a range of ailments, from the physical to the emotional. Similar healing trance dances are performed in different forms across North Africa, the Middle East, and in other countries throughout Asia. These healing modalities are based in the nonverbal, in the power of music and movement.

As a teen, when I came home after school, I headed straight to my room and closed the door behind me. I threw my backpack on the floor, and then moved out all my feelings, all my teen anguish of the day. I'd squeeze and push and contort my whole body, letting my feelings take over my movement. I called this my therapy. After five minutes or so, I felt better and would sit down with my books and get on with my homework.

Movement and dance can take the shifts that are in process through EFT, through your visualization and writing, through your forgiveness, and integrate it into the cells and tissues of your body. In my groups, I like to follow up the mental and emotional processes with movement. With hands on our heart, we'll sway gently to the melody and rhythm, surround ourselves with love or forgiveness, or reach our hands to the sky and draw down light to cleanse and renew our bodies. Or we might shake or fling our bodies in release.

You can do this too. Find your favorite songs that evoke or speak about release, empowerment, and moving on. As part of your healing processes, put the music on and dance!

Other Resources to Clear Your Stuff

I've just taken you through my own integrated model for clearing the fear. These practices are powerful, and, in my experience, they work. But they aren't the only ones available.

Not every modality is for everyone. Some people gravitate toward homeopathy. Others find it lacks substance. I have friends who swear by a practice called Transformational Breath. I explored it for a while and did receive benefits, but also found it physically uncomfortable. I concluded it's not for me. You, too, will need to find the healing modalities that are for you. You may have to experiment until you find the ones you resonate with and that work. Today we have a dizzying variety of psychotherapies, expressive art therapy, and body-centered therapeutic approaches to choose from. If you are drawn to a modality and find someone you love to work with, absolutely do it!

You can also create your own ritual for letting go. Elaine likes to spend time by a lake near her home. She described to me how for her release session she gathered a pile of rocks at the shore. One by one, she picked up each rock and spoke out loud what it represented to her. She acknowledged the parts of the circumstance that felt hard and found the words that needed to be said in order for her to feel complete. Then, with a blessing for moving on, Elaine tossed the rock into the glassy lake. A very fitting setting for letting go.

What kind of ritual would be fitting for you? Belinda, a poet, healed the relationship she had with her mom through poetry. If you're an artist, you can paint. If you like to take walks in the woods, you can commune with nature and talk to the trees. You can list the experiences you want to heal from on paper and burn the pieces in a backyard firepit. You can create a flotilla of branches and leaves to float down a river. Fling your arms wide and shout "I release you. I release you!" or smash a pile of pumpkins after Halloween.

You can make up rituals of all sorts. All the healing modalities we have at our disposal were made up by someone. The only limit to how you heal is in your imagination.

How to Know When You've Let Go

In biofeedback, a machine helps you identify when you have slowed your heart rate or reduced your blood pressure. As you watch a meter, you match that up with how you feel so you can continue or repeat it.

Although a meter is a nice tool, you don't need it to tell you how you feel. Focus your attention inward to notice the subtle or not so subtle emotional shifts.

Notice, too, if you resist or block the emotions as they arise. Sometimes, a simple awareness of tension will invite you to let go and experience a release through your body. Sometimes you'll encounter resistance to forgiveness. If resistance persists, don't make it an enemy. Just like fear, resistance is not something to be fought against, but rather honored and understood as there for a reason.

It may be that even with an explanation of what forgiveness is and isn't, you still have anger or resentment that you're not ready to let go of. Maybe that anger needs to be heard and to express itself. You may feel that by letting go, you will lose an identity that you forged for yourself around the experience. Or, you may feel undeserving of the freedom. It's so important to explore the resistance, because while the resistance is there, any attempt at forgiveness will be futile.

Ask yourself: *Why don't I want to let go of this? What will I lose if I let go?* And while you're at it, ask, too, *How long do I want to keep this resentment around? A day? A month, three years? My lifetime? Is this how I want to spend my precious time here on earth?*

Allow yourself the permission for it to take however long it takes. Keep an attitude of curiosity and experimentation to find what resonates with you and what works, what lightens the load.

When forgiveness feels complicated, it's likely to be part of a bigger emotional story. When that's the case, I suggest you address it with EFT, so you can unwind the pain and the story to arrive at a resolution. If you feel overwhelmed, don't hesitate to reach out to a coach or a therapist.

With these healing modalities, you will find that things you've held on to for a long time will loosen up and at some moment let go. Imagine you have a tennis ball in your hand and you want to release it. You loosen the tension in your grasp until, at last, it suddenly escapes from your fingers. Letting go isn't a "kinda" thing. You don't "kinda" let go of the ball. You let go when you let go.

When you resolve the past experiences, you'll feel a sense of relief, a detachment from your past, and a return to equilibrium. As one client recently described it, "I feel like I've caught up to myself."

After Maria's successful webinar, I asked her what it felt like on the other side of the work we did together. She said, "My fear used to be like a screaming child who took up all of my attention. Now it feels like we deactivated its potency. It's no longer active. We unpacked my stuff and put it away, and I can delight in myself now. I feel freer. And my pleasure is deep, even more so, because I know I had to work to get here."

If you take the time to declutter your psychic closet and resolve what you discover, you, too, will feel free of the past, a lightness of being, and ready to take on your next challenge with new energy.

You may wonder if you're completely done with the process forever. There is no clear-cut answer to that. You might or might not be, depending on the circumstances and stories of your life. That's perfectly okay, though. You're not going to discover all at once every circumstance about the past that limited you, nor do you need to. As you read through this book, new memories may get triggered. You'll likely say, "Oh my gosh, I forgot about that time I peed on my chair after school when I was six because the teacher told me not to disturb her under any circumstance. I had to go so badly but was scared to speak up."

Just bring your new memory back here to resolve and clear. As you resolve your stories and messages, instead of your past owning you, determining what you feel capable of, you will own your past and decide your future.

START WITH THIS

Close your eyes and place your hands over your heart. Find a way to connect with that younger you who felt small, diminished, hurt, misunderstood. Imagine you are wrapping your arms around littler you with love, understanding, and compassion. Spend a few minutes in this surround hug until she relaxes in your arms.

THE INNER
FREEDOM FRAMEWORK

PART 2

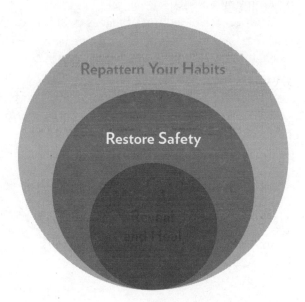

As I walked in my neighborhood one summer afternoon, I came upon two women chatting at the end of a driveway. One of these women held her young child, maybe two years of age. He seemed relaxed and calm, his head resting on her shoulder, a look of contentment on his face. It looked as though there was no place he rather be than in the arms of his mom.

Farther down the road, in another driveway, some kids chased one another in a game of tag, screeching and laughing. Around the corner, two preteen girls played music and were choreographing moves together, oblivious to me walking by.

Each of these scenes depicted children immersed in the moment, in a flow state. The kind of state that emerges when an environment feels safe. The children could be themselves, free and uninhibited.

The antidote to the feeling of fear is a feeling of safety. The sense that we can be ourselves, that we won't be judged, where we feel accepted, valued, and included.

In Part 2 of the Inner Freedom Framework, we'll look at how to restore the safety, from within you and around. First, you'll learn how to change your inner conversations to amplify the support you feel inside yourself. Then you'll examine how to create a welcoming environment for your moments in the limelight.

6

Transform the Inner Critic

"Feeling safe in someone's energy is a different type of intimacy. That feeling of peace and protection is really underrated."
VANESSA KLAS

"YOU'RE GOING TO screw up!"

"Stop it. I'm not!"

"Yes, you are. You know you will."

"Don't say that to me. I want to do a good job."

"Look at you! You're a wreck. Who do you think you are that you can pull this off? You're just going to embarrass yourself and hurt your reputation. I'm telling you, you're going to blow it. By the way, where are your notes?"

"Oh, shit, I left them at home."

"I told you you'd mess up."

Shayna relayed this conversation she had with herself on the way to a speaking gig.

"Say those things to me," I urged her.

"No. I can't do that," Shayna replied.

"Why not?"

"Because it's so mean and it's not true."

I paused and asked, "Would you say it to a client?"

"Absolutely not. My clients trust me to keep them safe and to protect them. It would be such a violation to hurt someone who is vulnerable."

I let Shayna's words sink into her awareness. If we wouldn't say those words to a client, if we wouldn't say certain words to someone we cared for, respected, and wanted to help, why do we think it's okay to speak to ourselves that way? If we wouldn't want to be around people who bully with that negative attitude and constant beratement, why would we tolerate it inside our own head? You essentially are carrying a bully around inside all the time. Do you feel safe around a bully? No!

Yet, this line of self-communication is rampant. In fact, every client I've had who wanted to overcome their fear of getting in front of an audience also had a robust and persistent inner bully.

Let's take a closer look at the beast and see what we can learn. Just like fear, the inner critic, too, can be cleared once and for all.

The Problem with Self-Criticism

When I was a girl, my mom used to tell me, "If you don't have anything nice to say, don't say it at all."

Did you get that message too? I grew up doing my best to be nice to others. I thought that how I spoke to myself was irrelevant. The way I saw it, as long as what I thought didn't hurt others, what I said inside my head wasn't a problem, right?

Wrong, of course. I didn't realize how damaging it was to have a negative internal dialogue. When you criticize yourself for how you show up to speak:

- You feel defeated and worn down. It's hard to feel good about yourself when you beat yourself up.

- You're not able to be present and focused.

- You inhibit yourself from naturally expressing yourself.

If you want to take a risk, ask for a raise, or step out onstage, this negative inner talk is the opposite of what you need. It makes you feel unsafe.

Don't work against yourself. It's scary enough to do something new or unfamiliar. When you put yourself in the limelight, more than ever, you need a supportive, encouraging environment that gives you a step up, a helping hand. You need a way to address that inner critic who will attempt to bum you out and stop you in your tracks before you even try.

I don't believe that we are condemned to live with an inner critic for life. In the book *The Continuum Concept*, Jean Liedloff described her time with an Indigenous tribe in the Amazon where there was, as she put it, an absence of unhappiness. Just think about that. An absence of unhappiness.

This startling observation radically challenged her ideas of human nature and our potential for well-being. It challenged mine too. It made me wonder: If we humans are not, in fact, programmed to self-criticize, what's the story with this nasty voice inside of us?

Several years ago, I did some research into positive psychology. In his book *Character Strengths and Virtues* (coauthored with Chris Peterson), Martin Seligman, director of the Penn Positive Psychology Center, outlined a list of twenty-four character strengths. I remember my surprise in seeing "judgment" listed among those strengths.

I've always tended to equate judgment with judgmental and to view it, therefore, as an undesirable quality. But seeing it included on Seligman's list of strengths made me wonder what I had missed in my understanding. Reading up on the concepts, I concluded that with judgment lies the ability to make considered decisions or come to *sensible* conclusions. To be judgmental is rather the opposite; you are quick to criticize without consideration.

In other words, you could say that a judgmental person doesn't show good judgment and someone who shows good judgment is rarely judgmental.

Could it be that our innate human capacity to judge well is hijacked by the traumas of our youth, when our capacity for wise judgment is not yet developed? That beneath the judgmental voice we hear in our head is the wise voice of judgment?

Imagine yourself at a tender age, when you first felt you weren't okay just as you were: you weren't acceptable or you were made to feel wrong. Maybe you grew up with someone who criticized and belittled you. Maybe you lived in a country or environment where it was dangerous to speak. Being the youthful, porous sponge that you were, you absorbed the criticisms and corrections from others around you—your parents, teachers, siblings, peers. If your parent forever called you a loser, you might resist it for a while, but at some point, you would start to believe it was true.

The inner critic may also have discovered that if you criticize yourself first, then if you hear it from another, it might not hurt so much.

In her book *Playing Big*, Tara Mohr proposes many creative ways to manage the inner critic. She also asserts that the voice of the inner critic will require ongoing management forever. That this voice in your head will find new and creative ways to harass you.

I'm not so sure. That's like saying that the way you communicate with others is fixed and can never change. That you'll talk to your boss or your mom or your kid only ever the way you've always done. Period.

In fact, we can grow in our communication skills with others. Yes, it can be a challenge. We may not know how to do it. But it is possible. We accept that there is value in learning to communicate effectively with others and it is something to get better at over time. I'm sure you've learned to speak more thoughtfully and kindly to those around you. You simply may have not put the same time, effort, and value into communicating effectively with yourself. It is possible. You just haven't put in the intention and awareness. Yet.

I can understand why it feels so fixed. Let's say you were eleven when you started to have negative thoughts about yourself. This young inner critic has the voice of a child, with the understanding and know-how of that age. And now you are an adult but with these same thoughts and self-talk habits from a much younger time, when you had fewer emotional resources. You haven't had the chance to mature that voice inside you to its full potential. Maybe no one has ever told you it was possible.

My daughter's words gave me a clue. She was seven and had pulled every puzzle, game, and toy out of the chest and the floor was littered. I blew up and went on a tirade about how dangerous it was to leave all those items everywhere and told her to *please* put it all away.

When I stopped for breath, she looked up at me with her big eyes and said, "Mommy, I hear what you're trying to say, but could you say it in a nicer way?"

Whoa. That was not what I expected. Her words caught me off guard and stopped me in my tracks. I let the hot air out of my balloon and said, "Why yes, honey, I can."

Her words of wisdom have stayed with me, and I think they are the perfect comeback to that negative voice in your head, a way to articulate how you want to be spoken to— with kindness: "I hear what you're saying, but can you say it in a nicer way?"

This is a beautiful beginning for change. Just doing this much will go a long way to create more inner peace. It's not just about changing the critic's voice in a superficial way, though. No, it has to be real and authentic. For that to happen, let's go deeper.

The Secret Life of the Inner Critic

Let's tune into a different voice for a moment—the voice that holds your deep desires. The one that wants to make an impact, to leave a legacy, to make a change, to contribute. What do you deeply desire in the impact you'd like to make? To be well regarded and recognized at work? To become a great keynoter, or a leader of a small movement, or a trailblazer who changes the world?

Believe it or not, the critic wants that for you too. Deep down, underneath all that sounding off, the critic wants the best for you too.

In his book *The Success Principles*, Jack Canfield correlates the manner of the inner critic to a parent who yells at their child when they run into the street without looking and then sends the child to their room in punishment. Although the parent appears to be angry, if you were to ask why he yelled, he would most likely say that it scared him to see his child run out in the street. What if a car had careened around the corner and his son was hit and killed? He couldn't risk the loss. He was worried and scared and needed to protect his child, and this was the way he saw to do it.

In this same way, the critic is concerned for you. All the parts of yourself are there for you to survive and thrive. Yes, the inner critic too. It just has a lousy way of expressing itself, most likely out of fear.

Let's say you can transform the harsh critic's voice into a kinder one, an inner enthusiast who is helpful, wise, and encouraging. Let's say you can have the voices inside you all on the same team and on your side. What would it feel like to have loving support that surrounds you with open arms whenever you fall down? Heavenly? A relief? Safe?

You can create that safe space within yourself, and in fact, it's critical if you want to feel safe when you put yourself out in the world without fear or hesitation. When you make a mistake, you need that safe space, to not feel hit when you're down. When you take a risk, you need that encouraging voice that says, "It's gonna be okay. I'm proud of you regardless of how it turns out!"

Right now, you and your inner critic are on opposite teams, dug into your positions. Although it would be big of the critic, she's not going to just come over to your side. Don't waste your time waiting around for that to happen. Sorry— you are going to have to make the first move (and the next and the next) to coax her out and make it appealing and safe.

Yes, you heard that right. If *you* want to feel safe, you need to make a safe space for your critic. It's tempting to think of the critic as being in the wrong, someone we need to fight against or to put in the back seat and not let at the wheel, as Elizabeth Gilbert suggests in her book *Big Magic*.

In *How to Talk so Kids Will Listen & Listen so Kids Will Talk*, Adele Faber and Elaine Mazlish share ways to be a "talkable parent." That means your child feels comfortable enough to tell you everything because they won't be judged, lectured, shamed, or blamed. Instead, they feel accepted, respected, safe.

Apply the same approach to the tantrum-pulling inner critic. Yes, allow the critic its space. Create an environment in which the inner critic isn't afraid to speak up, where it won't be criticized but rather listened to with interest and curiosity. Here's what we know:

- The inner critic really wants you to do well.

- It's there to protect you from shame, hurt, and rejection from others.

- It's really doing the best it can. It just has a lousy way of expressing itself.

- On the flip side of the harsh judge is the wise one with good judgment.

In order to transform the voice of the critic, first give her the space and vision for change. That is, begin to see what is possible.

I have a friend who had a reputation for not following through on what she said she would do. Whenever she offered to do something for the neighborhood crowd, it was met with skepticism. We didn't believe she would get it done.

One day she said, "Look, I'm really trying to change my ways, but if you see me only the way I have been, you keep me stuck in those old ways. So please let go of that image of me so I have the space to change into."

I was stunned by her words the way I was stopped in my tracks by my seven-year-old. She spoke truth. I was, indeed, holding her as unchangeable. Whether from us collectively holding this new space for her or by her own volition, she did indeed become a person of her word.

In this same way, even though the critic has acted or spoken in a particular way *forever*, give it the space to express itself in a new way.

The Inner Ally Process

Sometimes you'll have a thought, and you'll feel uncertain if it's a criticism or not. If you aren't sure, put it through what I call "The Best Friend Test." Say it out loud. If you wouldn't say it to a best friend, you know it's criticism.

At other times, our inner critical voice is unmistakable. In 2016, when I received the email that my first professional speaking reel was ready, I practically pounced on the link with excitement. The stage presentation had gone really well. I remembered all my words; I used the stage and I felt like I expressed myself freely. I could hardly wait to see the edited video to share around and start getting speaking gigs. I pressed play, and within seconds, my heart collapsed.

Then, I had an inner critic hissy fit. *Oh no! This is awful. I don't look confident at all! I look like a deer in the headlights! Ugh. That high cackle. Why did I make that huge gesture? So unnatural. Who let me wear that outfit? What was I thinking?*

I closed the tab and headed outside for a walk. When I returned, I turned my attention to other tasks and ignored the speaking reel. The days turned to weeks. This video, this talk that I had put so much time, effort, and money into, just sat there gathering digital dust on my computer.

On the one hand, I knew my message was important for people to hear. On the other, I couldn't stand to look at myself and didn't want anyone else to either. I told myself, "I have to look at this again." But how could I look at it when it was so painful?

I decided to use the Emotional Freedom Technique, the EFT tapping that I taught you in chapter 5.

Tapping on the outside edge of my hand I said, "Even though there's a part of me that's critical, I love and accept myself just as I am. Even though my shoes and white panty-hose look dorky, I love and accept myself just as I am."

After I repeated a few of these statements for what I hated in the video, I felt calm enough to watch it again. Then the idea came to me to write down every little thing I disliked, to let the critic go to town. After all, if the critic is loud, it must want and need to be heard, right? If it didn't want to be heard, why would it make such a racket?

I watched the speaker reel again and made a list of all the picky details. When I looked over what I wrote, something caught my attention. Almost everything on the list could, at some time in the future, be changed. Things like the way I said something, how I used my body, stuck my chin out, what I wore, etc.

There were also things that I couldn't change, like my physical features. I divided my list into two buckets: those things that could be changed and the things that would have to be accepted. I put my attention on the first bucket, those things that with some training, coaching, practice, and awareness can change.

Do you remember when I said that the judge actually has judgment? As I went down the list of nasty comments from my critic, I asked the critic, "Okay, if you don't like how I used my arms there, what would you have me do to make it better?" Then I let the previously "critical" voice start coming up with ideas. It started with:

Inner voice: "Why don't you go over those lines and see how else your body might want to gesture there."

Me: "Great. What else?"

Inner voice: "Why don't you video yourself doing it?"

Me: "Okay, I will. Thanks. Anything else?"

Inner voice: "Yes, why don't you try not moving at all and see how you like it."

You see, that judgmental voice inside? Underneath the facade is a voice with actual useful ideas.

I use this same process now in my program for getting comfy on camera. What is usually an onerous experience—watching yourself on video and cringing—becomes an opportunity to transform that inner critic into a helpful ally. Put that inner voice to work for you. Teach your inner critic a bit of etiquette, and it will become your inner enthusiast.

The Critic's Job Promotion

As you transform your inner critic, you'll need to update your name for her. After all, it won't do to lock in the critic by continuing to identify her as a negative part of yourself. Rather, try out some new role names that speak to what she is becoming in her new potential.

You can call her your inner coach, as Jack Canfield suggests. Or inner enthusiast. Some of the names my clients have come up with are inner being, inner wizard, hidden guide, inner artist, inner consultant, and inner soul. I like inner ally. Which one speaks to you?

Now you have a roadmap for addressing the places you want to improve. What about the stuff you disliked that can't be changed? We'll look at that in the next chapter.

START WITH THIS

What are the things you criticize yourself for when it comes to public speaking? Write a list. Then as you tap on the outside edge of your hand, say, "Even though there's a part of me that's critical, I love and accept myself just as I am." Go down the list and for each item say, "Even though..., I love and accept myself just as I am."

7

Heal Your Self-Image

"To be beautiful means to be yourself. You don't need to be accepted by others. You need to accept yourself."
THICH NHAT HANH

"IS THAT WHAT I look like? Is that the sound of my voice? Ugh!"

There's something about seeing or hearing yourself on video that feels foreign and disconnected from the way you think it should be. It's almost a given that you'll shudder at the sight of yourself. Even many professional speakers don't want to watch themselves on video. We addressed self-criticism in the last chapter, but how we feel about our appearance on camera runs so deep that it warrants a separate look.

Somehow, faced with the mirror, or video playback, we flip a switch to evaluation mode. We zero in on every detail we can find wrong in our appearance and mannerisms, according to us. It's crazy how preoccupied we can be with how we look on camera.

Unless, of course, you are a young child. Children are born with an enviable unselfconsciousness. My daughter and her three ten-year-old friends just loved to watch videos of themselves growing up. It was better than TV. They'd giggle and be enthralled with seeing themselves.

My guess is "enthralled" is not the word you would use to describe what it feels like when you see yourself on camera. More likely, it's torture. Beneath the torture, you might find shame. Shame that you don't live up to a certain type of beauty, a narrow and demanding view of beauty. A view of beauty formed by the values of the people around us, shaped and amplified by the culture and media.

Don't hold the illusion that people who fit your standard of beauty happily love themselves and their looks. Maybe some do. I certainly hope so. I can't tell you how many people have come to me whom others consider classic beauties who say that their top fear about speaking on camera is not liking how they look. It's well documented that many top models are equally self-critical, suffering from feelings of not being good enough and fear of losing their beauty in their twenties!

This self-rejection sucks out your joy. When you hate the way you look, you are essentially rejecting yourself. You're telling yourself, "I don't like you; I don't want you; I don't love you; I don't accept you." Would you ever say that to someone you hold dear? I don't think so. You are someone others hold dear. You are dear and deserve that self-affirmation.

This shame and rejection of yourself is also at odds with the part of you whose aim is to be seen and heard with a sense of ease and confidence. When you aren't comfortable or at peace with how you look, it inhibits you from being fully and freely yourself. You try to hide "in plain sight." Inhibition creates self-consciousness, which distracts you from being present and eats up mental bandwidth. It robs you of the pride and satisfaction you could have when you approve of, or at least accept, what you see.

Hey, I understand that you may prefer to look a different way. You may want to be thinner, buffer, younger, older, or have different features from those you were born with. I have my preferences too.

But holding yourself captive to an ideal of acceptability does not serve you, your objectives, or your audience. Just imagine if Oprah had decided that she couldn't go on the air because her weight wasn't where she thought it should be. What a loss that would be for the world! And yes, it's a loss for the world, too, if you decide you can't step out because your appearance isn't what you ideally would like it to be.

One of my clients grew up surrounded by women who criticized themselves as though it were sport. Not one of them could go a whole day without finding something wrong in themselves. Perhaps they wore their imperfections like a badge of honor.

Or maybe there is the worry that without self-harassment we won't feel motivated to make change. My mom was one of those people. She thought she was fat and told me so. "I hate how I look. Tomorrow I'm going on a diet." She said this, I kid you not, every single day of my life while I lived with her. It tore at my heart. I thought she was beautiful.

In *The Marvelous Mrs. Maisel* TV series, the main character, Midge, keeps a daily journal with the circumference measurements of her thighs, calves, and waist. I was horrified. But it made me curious to know if Mom, who was Mrs. Maisel's contemporary, had the same measurement routine. Rather than motivate Mom, this self-criticism seemed to have the opposite effect. I watched over the years as my mom, with her self-hate and tomorrow's diet, grew from a size 6 to plus sizes.

I wasn't surprised when I stumbled across a study conducted at the University of Massachusetts and McGill

University that followed hundreds of people who looked to achieve various goals, from job performance to weight loss. The study found that self-criticism made it less likely for people to achieve their goals. Rather, self-criticism left them demoralized.

Now, it's easy to say, "Get over yourself." It's harder to know how to go about doing that. I imagine that, given the choice, you would rather feel comfortable than uncomfortable about the way you look. Of course, why wouldn't you? Ideally, we all wanna feel the best we can about ourselves.

In the previous chapter, you learned how to separate what you dislike into separate buckets—those things you can change and those you can't. We can change our hair color or style it in a new way. We can choose clothes with colors that flatter. You can do these things with the enjoyment of adornment.

But many aspects of our appearance are not so easily changed. The shape of our nose, our eyes, our hips. Yes, theoretically we can lose or gain weight. We can buff up our body. We can have plastic surgery and dental work—and you might choose to.

For the time being, though, our facial features, our size—these things are fixed. So how do we find a better relationship, better thoughts, a better feeling for the things that can't be changed? We can borrow from how we deal with something else that can't be changed: the past.

Let's look at how the process we used for revealing and resolving past experiences can be applied here too.

To start off, I invite you to consider and write down your thoughts to these questions:

What features do you feel self-conscious about?
What do you feel they should look like instead?
Where do you think you got that idea from? A story or experience? The media?

When I asked this last question in my programs, I heard a range of stories—someone bullied for the color of their skin or a parent who told them, "You'd be pretty if your face was thinner."

One client shared how the women in her family bonded over beauty and gossip. She said, "That's how you fit in. My mom and my grandmother and my aunts would have plastic surgery parties, where one of them would get a procedure and everybody would spend the night at the hotel and order movies and food and stuff and have a good time and wine. I would go when I was little and was very used to seeing women's faces bandaged up."

Sometimes, you don't have an experience that happens to you directly, like Janet, who received definitive messages about what constitutes beauty in magazines, on TV, and with Barbie dolls and concluded she didn't meet that look.

When you have experiences like these, use the following steps to clear them:

1 Journal the experience, as you just did.

2 Tap with EFT.

3 Create a visualization with your fantasy helper for an outcome that brings you to wholeness.

4 Forgive and let go.

5 Dance into your self-love and appreciation.

You don't have to be a certain size or weight to have worthiness or to have the permission to say you are beautiful or beautiful enough. And when you get to that point of feeling okay in your skin, you can let go of it. You'll realize that in many ways it's irrelevant and not that big of a deal. People want to listen to you because it serves them in some way, and they like how you express yourself. How you do you. It's much less about how we look than how we think and the energy we bring.

Still not convinced? Read on. It may be that your mind needs to look at the issue from a different perspective.

Redefining Beauty

I used to dog-sit for friends when they went on vacation. One week, I had a cute little puppy with spots all over her. I was about to make a video ad for a program on healing our self-image when this dog rubbed up against my legs and stared at me with that "pick me up" look in her eyes.

As I held and petted her, I mused on how cute she was with her fun spots of colors here and there. I thought of how cats and dogs and goats and cows all come with interesting creative, unusual markings.

We, too, are similar in that we come into the world unique. Your uniqueness ties you genetically to the generations back who gave you your life. Consider your features as a gift from your ancestors that you can wear with appreciation as an emblem of your heritage.

Just think about it—each of us has our own combination of genes, right? Okay, unless you are an identical twin.

Twin or not, we each have this singular body that we get to experience this life with. Isn't that kind of wondrous and awesome? Like, I am me, I'm *"the* Linda Ugelow. This is my body that I get to live this life with." You are "the Sarah," "the Keisha," "the Michael."

And just as you have heard people say that no one else has your voice or what you bring to the world, no one else has you as a physical being, either.

Why not open your mind to the idea that we can celebrate and own our unique representation of our human species? What if, as with our animal friends, we adopted the idea of beauty being diverse and diversity being beautiful? What if you had *permission* to love yourself just as you are, and you didn't have to beat yourself up to fit into a mold?

Try this mantra: "I honor my face. I honor my body. I honor my lineage."

Your Love for Others Paves the Way

Often, the love and compassion we feel for others can model how we can be for ourselves. Think about how thrilled you are to see the people you know because of their special light, their love, their generosity, their sense of humor. They exude all the qualities that you love about them.

In one of my classes, I ask the students to pull out a photograph of someone they love. I ask them to look at the photo and write down all that they see and appreciate about this person in their face, their appearance, and their personhood.

When I look at a photo of my daughter, my heart swells. I love her eyes, her smile, the stray lock of hair across her face. I love how fun and funny she is, how she loves to make music and is totally into her friends and the outdoors. I love how she gets me out of the house to play with her, and how we also enjoy binge-watching on Netflix. I can go on and on just as you could, too, with someone whom you adore or admire.

Then I ask the participants to look at a photo of themselves and notice what they see. All of a sudden, a switch flips in their brain. Instead of seeing what they love, they see all the things they judge. It's so easy when you look at a picture of someone you love to list what you appreciate. How much more challenging it is looking at yourself! But I challenge you to do it. Look at yourself with the same loving eyes you use for others you care for.

What feature do you feel overly self-conscious about? Do you have people in your life with similar features? Does it make you love them any less? If your answer is no, let this be something to take note of—that maybe your teeth, your hair, your weight, do not make you less loveable or less valuable. Maybe what we see as flaws are irrelevant to the people who count.

There are people in your life who light up when they see you. They love what they see. You are someone that another person can go on and on about. You are someone's adored one.

Honor Your Body: Form and Function

There is a video on YouTube with more than 25 million views that tests your awareness. It's a short clip of basketball players, and you are asked to count the number of passes one team makes. While you're busy counting passes, a person dressed as a bear moonwalks across the court. Most people miss the bear because they're busy focusing on the players.

Maybe our full focus on our appearance also keeps us from awareness of something more intriguing and magnificent about our bodies: the body's function!

Contemplate this. We live in bodies that are magically "alive." What "alive" even means is a mystery itself. We inhabit these bodies that move, feel, regulate, heal. It's wondrous that we can hold a coffee mug, type on a keyboard, catch a ball, walk across the room. The magic is endless! Rather than bemoan the shape of your arms, steep yourself in the wonder that you can push yourself up off the floor, hug your child, or open a door.

Back in the seventies, I had a tiny book by Louise Hay called *I Love My Body* (it's out of print now). Each page celebrated a different body part with its remarkable functions. Do this with any and all parts of your body, but particularly with those parts you tend to criticize. For example: I love and appreciate my nose for drawing in and filtering the air as I breathe for the pleasure of fragrance of food and flowers. I love and appreciate my skin for holding me together and protecting my inner cells and tissues. For the pleasure of touch and eliminating toxins. I love and appreciate my teeth and lips for their ability to bite and chew my food. For their part to form words for speech.

When you find yourself falling into worry about your appearance, flip it around to love and appreciation for your body's function. Go deep into the details and see if you can't find yourself shifting your attitude to wonder. You get to have this body, and it's a gift. Celebrate and appreciate your gift.

You in the Mirror

My guess is that several times a day, you have a chance to see your reflection. Many of us use that time to evaluate ourselves with a critical eye: "Your hair is a mess. Look at those circles under your eyes; you look awful."

When we look in the mirror, we don't realize how negative we are or how it affects us. It's time to stop. Take a moment to think of how you'd love to be greeted by someone who loves you. Then go over to a mirror, smile at yourself, and say it. "Hey, love!" "Hiya, honey!" "Hello, gorgeous!" "Hello, handsome." "I love you. So nice to see you."

Every single time you see yourself, use a term of endearment. Take a moment to smile at yourself with warm appreciation. We've spent a lot of time dissing ourselves, and it's time to make up for it.

This practice particularly challenged me first thing in the morning, because truthfully, I'm not at my best when I roll out of bed. But hey, who is? I'd stagger into the bathroom, take a look in the mirror, and think, *Oh God, I look like shit.* One day, after playing with "The Best Friend Test" by saying my thoughts out loud, I caught myself in the act. "I heard that!"

I thought about how I greeted my daughter in the morning. She looked as crinkled and crumpled as the next person, but I had no problem giving her a loving morning greeting, like, "Hey, sweet pea!"

Talk to yourself this way too. Stumble into the bathroom and, as you peer out with your squinty eyes, say, "Hello, sleepyhead," or your endearment of choice. Speak to yourself the way you would someone you love. Let that someone you love be you.

Own Your Beauty

I travel to Hungary regularly with my husband to visit his family. On my first few visits there, I was struck by a particular energy in the Hungarian women I saw. Like here in the United States, the women in Hungary are of all shapes and sizes, of course, but what struck me was how the Hungarian women "owned" their bodies. They stood straight; their bodies looked relaxed and open. To me, they looked as if they knew they were attractive. These embodied, strong women showed themselves as beautiful, regardless of whether they were slender or large, young or old.

At the time, I was a size 6 and fit. However, inside, I felt completely different from how I viewed these women. I stood with my shoulders curved forward in a "please don't look at my breasts" kind of stance. Whereas these women stood with their chests open and proud.

These Hungarian women kindled a curiosity in me. What would it be like to embody that openness in my body? To assume I'm beautiful just by virtue of being human and alive?

What would it feel like to own "of course I'm beautiful!" with every cell in my body? What would that feel like to you?

Stake a claim in your own attractiveness—assume it to be true and own it. Define your kind of beauty and name it as the one you have.

I no longer think of beauty as something on the outside, that some people have and the rest of us don't. I've come to understand that beauty is not simply how we look. It has more to do with how we feel and how we allow it to radiate out.

I asked a group of students in my Comfy on Camera program when they felt most beautiful and what that felt like to them. Here's a sampling of their answers:

"I feel most beautiful when I am with folks I feel connected to. Where I allow myself to be fully myself without judgment and let myself express my emotions unencumbered. Feeling beautiful for me is about acceptance so I can really appreciate and swoon over how amazing I really am."

"I feel beautiful when I feel fully alive and I don't stop myself from flowing. I watched back a few of the videos, and thought I looked beautiful because I was having fun, I was expressing myself. And if I add makeup to that state, then it really enhances my beauty."

"I feel beautiful when I'm happy and present and I'm doing what feels good in my heart, regardless of how I look."

As Coco Chanel said, "Beauty begins the moment you decide to be yourself." This is what I want you to know. You are darling. You are beautiful.

START WITH THIS

Call on the universe with this loving-kindness prayer:

May I love and appreciate what I see in the mirror (or on camera), as do those who hold me dear.
May I see myself as having my own unique beauty.
May I radiate that beauty from the inside out.

8

The Power of
Positive Regard

*"The strongest force in our universe is
not overriding power, but love."*
CARL ROGERS

Y SISTER CALLED one January day.
"I know we planned this holiday together months
ago, but something came up at work for this weekend that I have to stay for. I'd like to send the boys down
to Florida without me. Can you be their mom until I come
down on Monday?"

"Of course," I answered, while inside my heart skipped
a beat.

I loved these two boys, but they were rambunctious and
wild, so different from my daughter who followed me like a
little duckling. I was at a loss on how to handle them, so I
turned to my friend Google for help. There, on the first page
of search results, a book caught my attention: *Transforming
the Difficult Child*, by Howard Glasser.

I found a copy at my local library and read it on the flight that night. Little did I know this book would forever change the way I look at people, at learning and being seen. The premise of Glasser's book is twofold:

- As children, we all want the attention or the energy of the other person. Ideally, we want positive energy, the kind that mirrors back the wonderful human specimens that we are.

- If positive energy is held back, the child goes for energy of any kind, even if it's negative.

The shift Glasser suggests to us as parents and teachers is also twofold.

- Stop looking at what isn't working, what you don't like, or what needs to improve. Don't give any energy to these things. Address negative behavior in a neutral to boring manner.

- Rather, look for the positive. Describe it with specifics and express your appreciation and/or what strengths you sense with enthusiasm.

Glasser related how this approach had made significant changes at a school in Arizona that had a yearly teacher turnover rate of 50 percent and eight times the number of school suspensions as other schools in the district. Within four years, teacher had attrition dropped to zero, just one child was suspended, and no children were diagnosed with ADHD.

The school went from the lowest in the district on standardized testing to excelling. Glasser says, "When children are led to feel great about who they are, they act out greatness."

With this new approach, the next few days with my nephews sounded like this.

"Look, you came in for breakfast all dressed and ready to go!"

"You fetched towels for us all. How thoughtful!"

"I love to see how you enjoy the pool. You could swim for hours, and you do!"

Though my brain was fried from the effort of looking at behavior with this new perspective and finding language for what I saw, the boys loved this mirroring, and our days were conflict-free.

I realized that this mirroring is not nourishment for only "difficult children." This is what we all need and how we thrive when recognized for our greatness. When we hear what works well, what is appreciated, what moves others, what others see as our strengths, capabilities, and expressions, we feel respected and esteemed; it is safe to be seen, safe to be heard.

Learning and Negative Attention

Some in our culture believe that in order to learn and build skills, we need feedback and correction of what's not right. More and more research points to the opposite: we actually learn best when we are recognized and when others reinforce and build upon what is already good.

Hearing critical feedback activates the fear center in the brain, the amygdala. When that center is activated, it impairs access to your cognition and perceptual awareness. When your attention is made to focus on what is weakest, especially when coupled with judgment, you're not inspired to learn.

Instead, learning is inhibited. Your brain responds to critical feedback as a threat and narrows its activity.

Similarly, when we find ourselves in an environment where there's no feedback, where people don't respond to us at all, it's easy to project what we think is going on—usually the worst. In contrast, when we have a sense of trust in the people around us, we feel held. They reflect the goodness of who we are. We are assured that we are okay, that the way we express ourselves is okay.

Sometimes when we've been wounded, it's hard to generate positive regard for ourselves. Our human development thrives from the positive regard from the family and tribe. It doesn't mean, though, that we are doomed, because in fact, there are many ways to create nurturing environments and to expand them to encompass more of our lives.

In his TEDx talk "The Validation Paradox: Finding Your Best Through Others," author Jeffrey Shaw suggests that because we see ourselves with certain negative self-beliefs, self-expectation, and self-limitation, others can often see more in us than we can in ourselves. Positive reflection can give us the reassurance we need to resolve some of the worries and doubts we carry about ourselves.

Create a Safe Space

Although the term "safe space" is used in many contexts today, I use it here to describe an environment in which you can feel most at home to express your true self. Where you can freely share your vulnerability, explore your self-expression, experiment, and be imperfect, all without fear of judgment.

Remember school? School was really not a safe space for me. In school I felt compelled to show myself at my most put-together, to take the fewest risks and make the fewest mistakes. Even "experiments" had to be controlled.

In a safe space, you can try things out and mess up. You can do real experiments and feel relaxed and curious. The reason is that in this kind of space, you have different objectives from those in school. School wants to grade and rate you, to quantify your performance. The objective of a safe space is personal growth, where you have the freedom to explore an aspect of a topic and see how it feels.

Improvisation (dance, music, stand-up, improv) does this. When you improvise, you accept what emerges as the material to explore. "Mistakes" are either incorporated into the exploration or let go of so you can move on.

For those of us who excelled in school, it can be difficult, even excruciating, to let go of "being good" at what we do. We'd rather not step into environments in which we don't already have competence.

I was at a conference where the speaker, Melissa Dinwiddie, author of *The Creative Sandbox Way*, asked us all to draw. A lot of people in the audience rolled their eyes as if to say, "Please don't make me do this. I'm a terrible artist!" But the point wasn't to be good. The point was to create a picture with a partner "conversationally." As you might expect, some of us judged ourselves through the experience: "I'm not as good as my partner. Oh, that looks stupid." Let me add here that the instruction for this activity was to create a monster. It could be any kind of monster—friendly, scary, weird. So it wasn't that we needed to make our drawing "pretty."

Speaking is much the same way. We think of eloquence as pretty. But don't we also respond to the raw, impassioned, and vulnerable? You don't get to where you want to go without a healthy dose of messing about.

Safe space is not about feel-good falsehoods. It's not a simple "pump up" like I used on Periscope: "Linda, you've got this; you're so good." Rather, positive regard offers authentic responses that reflect the truth of what people see in you and in what you create, where your strengths and best qualities are reflected back to you.

You can intentionally create a safe space by choosing what you include and what you keep out. Safety is created in groups when there is a shared value and intention not to judge—when you can trust you won't be criticized, evaluated, torn down, or made to feel different. Consider this when you look for practice environments for your public speaking.

The most powerfully creative and transformative spaces include these things:

- Unconditional friendliness toward yourself. This is the opposite of judgment. It contains curiosity and self-acceptance. It means a friendly attitude toward all that arises for you. You don't label anything bad or wrong; rather, you seek what is good. When this idea is promoted, you receive permission to provide it for yourself.

- Structured feedback from others that focuses on amplifying what's good, what resonates, what's powerful, strong, and compelling, what touches. There's no one way for this to happen. It's important to have rules, or a structure, though, and to follow them. If you give rules and don't follow them, it can feel like a breach of trust.

- Everybody counts. In many groups, some people take up more than their share of airtime, while others tend to hang out in the background. Especially as we're talking about being seen and heard, it's important for each person to have their time in the limelight. The use of a timer for certain activities creates a feeling of fairness. The group can also practice awareness of how much space each person takes to ensure everyone speaks.

* Time to reflect helps integrate an experience so it's not just one more blip in an otherwise busy life that goes by unprocessed. Take time to write and/or speak to make meaning out of it for yourself and tie it into your goals.

In my program Watch Yourself on Video Without Cringing, students watch themselves first with the eye of the critic, then, later on, with an appreciation for the things they see. As we saw earlier, looking for the good in yourself is much more challenging than looking for what's wrong. So, I ask people to help each other out. I ask participants to watch each other's videos and call out all the positives they see, all the things they like and appreciate about the person in the video—for example, their energy, delivery style, and qualities and essence they radiate.

As Terry, one participant, put it, "This opens a whole new way of getting to know and love myself better. You realize that all the things you may have been focusing on are not what others see."

Yes, that's true. You realize that you come across as more compelling, focused, joyful, warm—fill in the blank—than you could see in yourself.

We are limited in how we see ourselves. Others can see things we don't. You might have an immediate reaction to this as you read and think, *Oh no, I don't want people to see my flaws.* But when our flaws are visible, when we are loved and embraced in spite of them or even because of them, that is a balm for the soul. When we discover that, for other people, many of our flaws go unnoticed, we too can let go of so-called "imperfections."

The Toastmasters Question

Toastmasters is an international organization that promotes speaking skills. Lots of people find Toastmasters helpful. In Toastmasters, you'll find some elements of safety. There is support and encouragement, a commonality among the members who want to become better speakers, and maybe some shared anxiety around speaking. There is also a grading system, where you are rated on how good you are according to some standards that someone in the audience checks off.

As you recall, evaluation and the fear of not making the grade can light up the fear center in the brain. Just imagine having someone sitting in front of you in charge of counting the number of "um's" you say in your talk. This "um" counter is meant to make you more aware. It might. But it can also make you more self-conscious, tense, and worried. I'll give you another way to deal with "um" in chapter 12.

I don't bring up this potential pitfall in Toastmasters to bash them. I know many people who attribute their speaking confidence to their years of attending a Toastmasters group. I've also worked with clients who were simultaneously in Toastmasters and who benefited from coaching with me on the side.

One client, Susan, struggled to feel comfortable in her local group. She felt afraid, and people confirmed that she had the look of a deer in the headlights. That made her feel even more self-conscious, and her fear of looking fearful made it hard to improve her skills.

After she and I worked together for a few sessions, her classmates at Toastmasters commented on how she had changed. She seemed more relaxed and confident, and her speech had more power and impact. Well, yes, because she had let go of the fear. She was now grounded and present. Without her fear, she could now benefit from the training they provided. And she could tolerate the evaluative vibe of the program. She filtered the feedback—let in what was useful and let the rest slide by. Two years later, she informed me that she had become the Toastmasters director for her region.

The Leaky Bucket Fix

It's wonderful to have people tell us they love us, appreciate us, respect us, or like our work, creativity, or cooking. It's a real boost of dopamine. It gives us the message that we belong and are significant. At least for a while. When we are wounded, however, and we feel we aren't good enough, this lack can create a craving that never feels satisfied. We seek out endless positive feedback from people. When we get some, it feels good for a while, and then we need another fix. This issue is never resolved because our younger self inside is still hoping, wanting, needing to get approval from the person we didn't get it from in the first place.

If you resonate with this, it's an opportunity to look more closely at the message. Where in your life did you crave positive regard from others? Who did you desire to please but couldn't? Take what you uncover here and resolve it with the clearing modalities in chapter 5.

Now let's turn our attention to the positive regard we do get.

Arrogance Versus Self-Love

One snowy afternoon, my friend Eliza surprised me with a visit to my home. When she walked in, her face lit up.

"Oooo, I love your sweater!" she exclaimed.

"Oh, this?" I looked down. "It's kind of stretched out and the sleeves are frayed."

"Linda!" Eliza interrupted me sharply. "If someone gives you a compliment, simply say 'thank you' and keep it at that."

"Thank you," I repeated obediently. And I smiled at her with deep appreciation, for in this one instant, she had solved a problem I didn't know I had—how to comfortably accept compliments.

If you are like most people, when someone tells you, "You look great today!" you respond with, "Oh God, I haven't washed my hair," or "I've got bags under my eyes from lack of sleep."

Isn't it interesting? We want to feel seen and appreciated. We want other people to share what they like about the way we look, about what we say and do. But then when it happens, we tend to deflect and minimize. We push away the very thing we say we want!

I was chatting with my friend Julia, a photography major at college. I told her I appreciated her artistic perspective and how creative she was. Without missing a beat, she said, "Oh, I'm not, really."

"Why do you say that, Julia?" I asked.

"Oh, because I'm so aware of how much more there is to learn. And I really admire the great artists around me and don't think I'm as good as them. And, I guess, I feel it would be immodest to agree with you."

Why do we deflect compliments? Why is it so hard to receive them? Just like the messages we absorb around being seen and heard, we also pick up mixed messages around receiving praise and compliments. Modesty would be at the top of the list. Like Julia, I grew up thinking that it was considered good etiquette and a sign of modesty to deflect compliments. I supposed that it would make others feel more comfortable around me if I minimized myself.

Sarah, a student in one of my courses, brought up a related concern. "I'm uncomfortable hearing nice things about me because it feels really close to being arrogant, and I was taught that arrogance was bad. In fact, we used that word as an insult. We'd say, 'Oh, that person is arrogant,' and we don't want to be like that. Right?"

Right. We don't want to be arrogant. But what we were told as kids was misleading and incorrect, and this is why: Arrogance is the opposite of positive self-regard. Arrogance is an inflated sense of self. You puff yourself up to compensate for your lack of self-esteem or self-love.

Positive self-regard, however, is kindness toward oneself and a belief that you are okay just as you are, with your flaws as well as your talents. You don't turn to arrogance because you are fine with who you are. When you are filled with self-love and compassion, when you have what you need, you actually have more capacity to focus on others, like your audience and their needs.

Yes, You Are Deserving

Now, it could be that you deflect compliments because you believe you deserve praise only when you achieve a certain standard of perfection, like an A grade in school or an award. But when you think about it, everything in a process leads to the next level. That means any point in a process can be looked at with the pride of accomplishment. Of course, you will grow and get better. Of course, there are others around you who may have more experience. That will always be the case. The point is that you can receive kudos at any stage. You don't have to be the best in your field for others to appreciate you. Don't push appreciation away. Take your blessings as they come.

I don't want to gloss over the subtext or inner dialogue that goes along with this deflection. In your mind it might sound like, "I'm not that good. I don't know what I'm doing," or "If they only knew how little I know, they'd be horrified." Would they? Or is this your own self-assessment? Is this the inner critic piping up? Would you say these words to someone you admired and cared for?

Darrell struggled to receive compliments. When we dug into his resistance, it turned out to be guilt for some past behavior. He had copied his friend's homework in second grade and turned it in as his own. He continued to punish himself all these years, in part by depriving himself the gift of receiving positive regard from others. He didn't feel deserving.

If you feel shame for something in the past, if you feel that you are undeserving of positive regard because of it, that's exactly the time you need tender, loving arms around you. Take time to explore the core of this belief, that you are undeserving, and clear it away using the techniques in chapter 5.

Not too long ago, thinking highly of yourself or your circumstance or family was believed to draw the attention of the evil eye. My grandmother Molly used to pretend to spit— *"pooh, pooh, pooh"*—if one of her friends said, "What beautiful grandchildren you have." This was to protect us from the evil eye, whose prime responsibility was to keep a lookout for excessive love, admiration, and appreciation.

Who came up with this idea that we should be afraid of compliments and admiration? Who decided it was dangerous and undesirable? Might it have been a way to keep certain groups of people fearful and disempowered? I don't know the answer, but this I do know: You deserve to bask in the warm surround of appreciation. You deserve to be held.

The Energy of Receiving

We've been focusing here on the experience of the receiver. There is another side too—that of the giver. When someone offers you a compliment, a reflection of some essence or appreciation, it's a kind of gift.

When you don't receive it, if you take a look at it and drop it on the ground and say, "Nah, that's not me; it's not true," or "Doesn't matter," you not only put yourself down, you also bring down the giver of the gift. When we push others away along with their positive regard, we maintain a division or wall between them and ourselves. You see a lot of people onstage doing this. They finish a talk and when people applaud, they break away and make a run for backstage.

In contrast, when you receive, you allow the wall to come down. You let yourself be seen and appreciated. When you stand onstage and all eyes are on you, the audience is giving you a gift, the gift of their attention. How do you take it in? How do you receive it?

You can say, "Oh, this? This isn't all that interesting. My words aren't well put together. My speech is a little frayed around the edges." Or you can open your arms and say, "Thank you!"

After my Watch Yourself on Video workshop that I mentioned earlier, participant Terry further shared how it felt to receive positive regard from others. He said, "I'm leaving here with an expanded sense of self-acceptance. Instead of the critical inner voice that isn't echoed anywhere else in my world, only in the space between my ears, I'm opening to see myself with the loving eyes that my friends would see me with."

How you receive compliments from other people can expand your self-acceptance and impact your speaking confidence. It will boost your ego in the best of ways. It will empower you. Don't be afraid of this power. Own it and you will build your capacity to delight in the limelight.

You Are the One You've Been Waiting For

As lovely and impactful as it is to receive positive reflections from others, you can see that it all comes back to how much you allow yourself to take in and receive. Ultimately, you are responsible for your inner experience.

I attended a weekend spiritual workshop a few years ago. There was one message: no one can fill you up 100 percent of the time. Not your parent, child, sibling, friend, teacher, mentor, or client. They may really, really want to be there for you 100 percent of the time, but they simply can't. They have a responsibility to themselves and to others in their lives.

There is, however, someone who *can* be there for you 100 percent of the time. Someone who is on call twenty-four seven. And that person is you. You have the capacity to be your biggest supporter, your kindest coach, your staunchest advocate. Dedicate yourself to being that person.

Your Daily Practice of Positive Regard

In the previous chapter, you changed how you speak to yourself in the mirror. You offer your reflection a warm greeting: "Hey, champ!" "Hey, beautiful!" "Hey, sweetie!"

Before I go to sleep, I review my day. I find five things I feel proud of from the day or that I appreciate about me. This forces me to look for the good. I then list five things that I forgive myself for. It could be items on my to-do list that I didn't get to, or how I handled myself in a conversation. This allows me to release the stress from the day and practice letting go. I top it all off with five things I'm grateful for, because gratitude connects me with the world around me. I suggest you try this out too. You can write them down in a journal, review them in your head before your evening meditation, or share them as a family ritual. You'll end each day feeling cleansed, renewed, and grounded in the present moment.

START WITH THIS

It takes commitment to be consistently kind. If you give yourself permission to be bolder and take risks, it wouldn't be fair to then get mad at yourself if something doesn't turn out as planned. That wouldn't be honest permission-giving. Make a promise to be there for yourself no matter what. Write a love letter to yourself stating your intentions. Say something like:

"Dearest [your name], I promise to be on your side, to look for the best in you, to find words of encouragement, and to support you and celebrate you as I would my dearest friend. I give you permission to step out. You are safe with me. I have your back."

Sign it and keep it where you can read it from time to time.

THE INNER
FREEDOM FRAMEWORK

PART 3

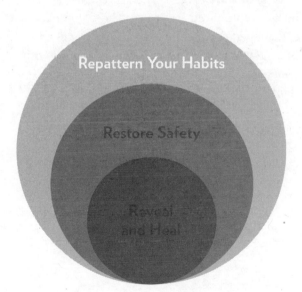

Repattern Your Habits

Restore Safety

Reveal
and Heal

"Repatterning" is a fancy word for learning things that will become your new habits. When you've been living your life in a particular way, how you express yourself becomes a pattern in your neurophysiology. You may carry tension in your throat from years of speaking in a whisper or shouting over siblings to be heard. During those years when you were in fear, you became used to protecting yourself. Fearful thoughts pull back your energy and tighten your body.

In Part 3, we'll look at some patterns of thinking that you may be holding on to that keep you concerned. Next, we'll explore your presence, down to how you breathe and relax, and how you use your voice. You'll learn ways to practice expressing yourself so that you feel you bring your authentic self with you wherever you go. And finally, we'll look at the peak experience waiting for you as a public speaker.

You can replace old habits that hold you back with new habits that open you up and expand your inner experience. It is in this new way of being that you fall in love with expressing yourself, with communicating and delighting in the limelight.

9

Reset Your Mindset

"We can't wait for the world to confirm who we are, or we'll always be asking permission to exist."
SARAH MONTANA

ABITS OF THOUGHT, or the way you think, can keep you in a straitjacket. We have a mountain of unconscious attitudes and beliefs that we absorb as true. These things sneak into us and latch on as we move through the world. We assume these ways of thinking are necessary in order to stay safe or belong to the tribe. We assume they keep us liked and respected.

At one time, you might not have wanted to make waves, and it might not have been prudent to do so, but now you do. Now you want to stand out and be a standout onstage. You want to be seen. To do that, you need a different rule book from the one you've been using. And guess what? You get to write the rules! The rule for the rules is that they have to give you the widest possibilities for you to expand into your potential.

In this chapter, I'll go over some of the common obstacles in our thinking that have been passed down to us from previous generations. They no longer serve us, and they keep us afraid to step into the fullness of ourselves. Just as we carry around old experiences and memories, we carry around old concepts until we hear them put in a new context. You've already discovered that fear is a message of something deeper and that you can heal the voice of your inner critic.

I want to help you come up with better ways of thinking about more things—"better" meaning you'll feel more relaxed and at ease being in the limelight. Because how you see something is how you experience it. It can be the difference between struggling and thriving.

Keep a lookout as you read for remnants of the psychic closet. You might find you have a story inside that wants to come out to the light. Keep a notebook to jot it down and promise to give it some space.

Permission

Because we are rule-bound in our unconscious, in order to step out of our own rules, we need to create new ones. It all starts with giving ourselves permission.

After Brené Brown published her book *The Gifts of Imperfection*, Oprah hosted an online journaling workshop with Brené that I joined. On day one, we created permission slips for ourselves. Remember the permission slips you got from your parents or teachers at school so you could miss a program or take a bathroom break during class? They're like that, but more creative.

In the workshop, we made journal art. I pulled out water-colors and painted some blocks of color on the journal page to represent scraps of paper. When the page dried, I pulled out some colored markers and wrote down passes I felt I needed at that time.

Permission to:

Take big risks.
Mess up big-time.
Forget things.
Slow down.
Be "behind" and know it's okay.

When I look at these passes today, they still feel relevant. If you were to make a list of permissions, what would they be?

Beginner Bliss

Some people have a super-hard time being a beginner. It feels humiliating to let go of competence. In school, though we are told we're there to learn, the unspoken text says something different. It says, "Yes, you are here to learn, but it's even better if you already know the answers or at least can pick them up fast." As kids, we learn that it's shameful to be slow, to not "get it."

What can we do to take away that shame of being a beginner? Learning new things can and should be applauded, but only if we can leave off the shame when we're new to the game. Of course, as a beginner you won't be as good as you'll be later on. It's the plain truth. You can't get better if you don't start from the beginning.

Let's have a look at children again for inspiration. Children don't have a hard time as beginners. When my daughter was six, some of her friends took up the Suzuki method for violin. Their first recital always began with the same piece: "Twinkle, Twinkle, Little Star." These little budding musicians all stood with poise and delight at their first accomplishment. Every six months, I marveled at their improvement. After two years, I was blown away. I remember thinking, *Wow, so that's how you learn to get good on an instrument. Study, practice, and consistency.* But what really stood out for me was how happy they were with themselves.

Wherever you are in your journey, you may feel like you should be someplace else, further along, better than you are, more established. Don't fall into this trap of needing to be better. Of course, you could be better, and you will be! We are all always growing and improving when we have the intention to grow and improve. Anyway, you can't be anywhere else than where you are. You can't be where you ain't. You can't be further along, more experienced, more knowledgeable.

In his book *A New Earth*, spiritual teacher Eckhart Tolle suggests that we resist being in the present moment by fighting "what is," and that fighting with "what is" causes struggle and suffering. In other words, when you tell yourself you should be somewhere you're not, you suffer. When you stop resisting the present moment, when you can accept and be open to where you are, then you feel at peace.

While writing this book, I remember thinking, *Linda, you are so slow.* I paused and wondered, *Is this a mean inner critic thought?* So, I put it through "The Best Friend Test" and said it out loud with the name of someone I cared for—my daughter. "Lexi, you are so slow."

Nope. I wouldn't say that. In fact, if Lexi came to me worried about being slow, I would ask questions, starting with, "According to whom? Whose timeline are you on? Whom are you trying to prove yourself to?"

And I'd look for ways to reframe it as well. Because we are the way we are for real reasons. If you're slow, maybe you're still formulating your ideas. Or maybe other things are going on that need attention. Maybe you need more information to move forward. There is nothing wrong with and everything beautiful about meeting yourself where you are.

When you allow yourself to be in the present and accept where you are as not just okay but also wonderful, you'll experience more joy and accelerate the changes in you. All will happen in good time. You can't push the river.

If you've never made a video, if you've never given a talk and you want to start, there is no shame in being new! Let yourself delight in it, just like the children playing "Twinkle, Twinkle" on the violin. Say to yourself, "I am just where I am, and I honor that. There is nowhere else for me to be." This is radical self-love.

Self-expression is not something you can grade. There is no right or wrong way to express yourself. Rather, expanding your self-expression requires a large degree of risk-taking and freedom to explore. Build your capacity to tolerate and embrace imperfection. Understand that it's just as important to learn what doesn't work as it is to learn what does. Do you remember the game Twenty Questions? You get as much good information from the nos as from the yeses.

In research and development, labs typically have shelves of their failed experiments alongside the ones that worked. It's not about good or bad. It's all about gathering information. In truth, all of life is one big experiment. This is especially true as you play around with self-expression.

Let experiments be led from a place of curiosity rather than critique. This means you have to promise to be impeccably nice to yourself. Promise not to beat yourself up or put yourself down. Don't be the biggest obstacle to your own growth! Learn instead to be your number one fan.

The Envy Trap

It's easy to look at others and compare ourselves to them. This is why it's so important to acknowledge where you are in your process. Honor your own journey and know that there is no one else on it, no one else in your lane. You have your own unique path on your way to personal fulfillment.

That said, envy is a powerful emotion, and if you dismiss it, you may miss out on an important opportunity. Just like fear, rather than push away jealousy, let's get curious and investigate it.

Envy awakens our desire, and our desire is key to our motivation. When you feel envious of another person, take a moment to uncover what about them or their circumstance you would like for yourself. Is it something about how they present themselves, or that they have a strong online presence? Would you like a loyal following too? Or the support of a business team like they have behind them?

Make a list of all that you would love to have for yourself. Read the list out loud, prefacing each line with "I desire to..." For example: "I desire to be a sought-after podcast guest," "I desire to be natural on camera, to speak with ease and fluency, to get paid to speak." Add why you desire each thing to ensure it's a true desire that aligns with who you are and your purpose.

Take a moment to enjoy the burn of desire inside you. Feel, too, your determination to make it happen—in your own time, of course. Envy is a gift and an opportunity when you take it in the right perspective.

Likability

I used to think that the measure of my value as a person was that everybody liked me. Maybe it came from observing how all the "cool" kids in school seemed to have a large following. I thought and hoped that if I was nice to people, they would like me. I don't know if this idea was literally said to me at some point or if I somehow sussed it out. Wherever this came from, it's off the mark. If you are standing onstage and hoping that everyone is going to love you, you're setting yourself up for a lot of needless suffering.

Think about your own experience viewing others. I'm sure you don't find every presentation equally relevant to you. You have your preferences. There are speakers who have blown you away or whom you've felt connected with, and others, well, not so much. I know without you telling me that there are videos you watch from beginning to end and others you don't. But just because you or I may not want to watch or listen to a particular person, doesn't mean they aren't worthy or that others don't derive tremendous benefit from them.

I'm the first to admit that I'd love for everyone to want to watch me and love me. It's unlikely to happen, though. I don't believe there's a single person on earth, no matter how virtuous they may be, whom everyone likes. Not Oprah, not Nelson Mandela, not Seinfeld. Even gods and goddesses don't have universal appeal. So, give that one up.

Besides, it's not relevant or necessary to be loved by all to make an impact. It's okay that not everybody will want to watch or listen to me. It's just something I have to let go of, and you do too. If you want the freedom to have your preferences, you have to allow others to have theirs. Let go of the belief that you need 100 percent likability in order for you to be okay.

Instead, appreciate that you appeal to those wonderful folks who are for you. And don't worry about the rest. Give yourself permission to be okay with that. Put yourself out there regardless. Your people are waiting for you.

See Your Past as a Boon

No one's past is all bad. And not even the bad stuff is all bad. If you have survived your past, which you obviously have done, then you are already resourceful! You've learned skills that came directly out of your experiences. You may be a great listener whom people trust with their deepest secrets. Maybe you know how to set boundaries and not let others derail you. Maybe you have a capacity for introspection, or you have the ability to deal well with difficult personalities everyone else avoids at work. Maybe you have a desire and determination to do things differently from your parents and teachers, to keep whatever happened to you from happening to others.

See the burdens of the past as things that make you who you are today in the most positive way.

Other People Don't Always Know Best— Even Teachers and Mentors

Don't assume other people always know what's best for you or have your best interests in mind. When I was in grad school in the Expressive Therapies department, I wrote a manual on the practice of Authentic Movement. It was a guide for groups about how to use movement for personal growth and spiritual development, and to source their creativity. I was excited to publish it.

I showed the finished copy to someone I had studied Authentic Movement with, someone I considered one of my mentors, and asked her what she thought. "Oh, I don't think you should publish this," she said. "I don't think people should be encouraged to practice this on their own, without a trained leader."

I deflated on the spot. I had truly expected her to offer some positive feedback on my accomplishment and wasn't prepared for this discouragement. Crestfallen, I put the beloved manual that I had worked so hard on back on the bookshelf, where it collected dust.

Years later, I told the story to a friend. She was apoplectic about it. "Don't you see, Linda, she was jealous of you!" The thought had, in fact, occurred to me, but somehow, I took my mentor's voice as the voice of authority. I sometimes wonder what would have happened if I had gone ahead and published the manual. But at the time, I couldn't have done it differently. I couldn't imagine risking her disapproval. Even though I never saw her again.

I see my inability to go against my mentor's pronouncement as related to our educational system. We are schooled to believe that we need others to tell us if we are okay. If our writing is okay. If our ideas are okay. In school, everything we create for six hours a day runs through an evaluation system according to some outside expert's opinion. We learn to not trust ourselves or be self-reliant in our self-assessment. We aren't taught to make our own decisions. We get hooked on the approval trap.

Here's the conundrum. You want to stop giving up your inner authority to others, but you also need help to learn what you don't know, like how to give a better talk or write a better book. How do you tease this apart and find a balance with it? Here's what I recommend.

Learn what you can from teachers, try out the things that are suggested, but run it through your filter to decide if it's right for you. Listen to the feedback from your audience so you can continue to understand their needs. Keep what resonates with you and discard the rest. At some point, we have to graduate from external validation. I'm saying this as much to myself as to you. Trust yourself to be the expert of your own experiences. You are the decider. It's your journey.

Speaker's Remorse

Have you ever had a conversation with somebody and afterward kicked yourself for saying something you wish you hadn't, or for not saying something you wish you had? I call that conversation remorse. I used to feel that all the time, and a nagging sense of shame would follow me.

The same thing can happen when you give a talk. Even with the best of intentions to be prepared, sometimes you're not. Or maybe you were but the unexpected happened and threw you off your game. After you're done, you start kicking yourself for something you did that you wish you hadn't or what you forgot to do that you wish you had. You miscalculated your audience. That exercise you planned didn't go so well. Maybe you didn't make the impression you had hoped to and you feel that you lost status in someone's eyes.

Jenisse felt honored when a friend invited her to speak at an event. She was an aspiring speaker and had some experience under her belt, but not a lot. She believed that this event would take her to a new level of leadership. She wanted to impress her friend and gain new clients. At the event, Jenisse felt nervous and told the audience so. She thought that calling attention to her nervousness would make her feel more comfortable, but it didn't. The talk went fine, but not great. Nobody signed on as a client, and her friend was polite but not gushing, as she had hoped. For Jenisse, it was one big disappointment. She decided that the talk she had prepared was too elementary, that she must be a bad speaker, that she was just not good at this. She wanted to crawl into a hole and never speak again, so great was her internal angst.

These feelings can be pretty painful and can pursue you for days, months, or years if you don't address them. Something like this can become one of the impacting experiences you've been working to clear by reading this book, so don't let it go by without unpacking what happened. You need to be your own biggest advocate during these difficult moments.

It is likely that you will, at some point, have speaker's remorse. It's easy to get discouraged and pull back into your shell. But you won't do that, will you? Because you know that your message, your purpose, is bigger than any setback. When you experience speaker's remorse, pull yourself together and follow the Inner Ally process with a few modifications:

1 In a journal, describe the circumstance as if you are writing it down like a reporter.

2 Make a list of all the things you fear and feel bad about.

3 Tapping on the outside of your hand, go down your list and say out loud, "Even though I wish that... I love and accept myself just where I am." Alternatively or in addition, forgive yourself for each little and big thing. Actually say, "I forgive you for [insert whatever it is]." Forgive yourself for not being faster, further along, more experienced, more perfect. Forgive yourself for being so unforgiving.

4 Make a new list of all the things you can be proud of, that you can appreciate about your talk and yourself for doing it. This will awaken your self-compassion and wisdom.

5 Engage the help of your Inner Ally by asking for suggestions of what to do differently next time. With each suggestion your Inner Ally makes, say, "Thank you, what else?"

6 Write a letter to yourself. Begin with "This is what I want you to know." Include words of wisdom, things you want to remember, promises of how you want to be there for yourself in the future.

When I run this workshop, many participants share how they've been ruminating about a particular presentation for four or even twenty years. After doing this process, Tara said, "I feel light. I let go of the 'could have, would have, should have.' I'm more purposeful now and have my list of what I'm going to do differently so I can achieve the results I want in the future."

Remember this too. There is so much more to come! The more speaking you do, the less significance each event holds.

For this reason alone, line up several speaking engagements close together. This way you can give yourself over to the speaker's journey. You give yourself permission to be in process, always growing and learning. You may wish you were further along. You may wish you were more experienced. I've said this before but it's worth saying again and again. You can't be where you ain't.

Fiercely honor where you are. Greet each stage with open arms. Reflect and learn from whatever happens. If you honor where you are at each stage of the game, you can enjoy the process of unfolding. That is in itself a joy—the joy of becoming more of who you are. And that remorse you felt? It will make a good story you can tell later.

Mistakes and Glitches

My friend Cathy, who lived across the street from me growing up, loved to dance as much as I did. We often took classes together, and in our early teens we choreographed duets to perform at the annual Temple revue. One year, we used the Motown tune, "Get Ready." It was simple choreography, where we did the same steps at the same time.

On the first night, right in the middle of our performance, I completely forgot the sequence. So I started to improvise. I mean, the show must go on, right? Cathy glanced over at me and when she saw that I was not in step with her, she stopped, put her hands on her hips and said, "Linda, *what* are you doing?"

She was a year older than me, so acting like the big sister was completely in character. I turned and danced with my back to the audience so they couldn't see me stage whisper, "I forgot the steps. Keep dancing!"

The point here is that the audience has no idea what you planned, only you do. Many mistakes are known only to you, unless you announce them to the audience. Think ahead to address the mistakes and glitches you are likely to have. Here are some of the mistakes you may be afraid of making as a speaker:

- Skipping a section or "messing up" the order. You're happily going along and suddenly you realize you just left out a section. What to do? It may be that what you were going to say isn't crucial and you can just let it go and move on. But maybe that section is necessary for the audience to understand what comes next. You can stop and say, "Wait, before we go any further, I want you to know X." Or you can do like me and improvise for a bit to find the spot where the information can slide back in.

- Stumbling over your words. If you stumble over a word or sentence, please don't make it a bigger deal than it is. We all stumble. Laugh, or simply repeat it and move right on. Famed Broadway star Idina Menzel said, "There are about 3 million notes in a two-and-a-half-hour musical; being a perfectionist, it took me a long time to realize that if I'm hitting 75 percent of them, I'm succeeding. Performing isn't only about the acrobatics and the high notes: It's staying in the moment, connecting with the audience in an authentic way."

- Going off script and rambling. When you notice this is happening, rein yourself back in and put a period on it as soon as possible. Pause and move on to your next point. This switch from your ramble to organized thought will create a dynamic change in your delivery that will feel masterful.

- Forgetting what you were going to say. Michael Port, author of *Steal the Show* and co-founder of Heroic Public Speaking, offers some creative options for when you are speaking to an audience and forget what you are saying. For instance, you can take a long, thoughtful pause as you peruse the audience. No one will be the wiser that you are thinking about what to say next. In fact, you'll give the audience a break and let them digest what they just heard. You can also repeat your last words to get you back on track. Or get a drink of water to buy yourself time. You can even ask the audience, "Where was I just now?" They'll enjoy helping you out.

Making mistakes can have a plus side. It can make you more relatable. Who doesn't love a good blooper reel? I once gave a talk using the slides to remind me of what I wanted to say. (I've since learned that experienced speakers don't rely on their slides, but I didn't know that at the time.) As I was reviewing my deck in the morning, I added in an extra photo that perfectly illustrated the point I wanted to make. When the photo came up during the talk, my mind went blank. It was a photo of a desk with papers all over and a spilled cup of coffee. What was the point I wanted to make?

I turned to the audience and admitted my quandary.

"I can't for the life of me remember why I put this slide here." (That was another rule I broke—don't show the audience that something is wrong.)

The audience waited for what I would do. Would I remember? Would I give up and move on? Either way it would have been fine. However, I knew I had a good reason for the slide, and it bothered me to skip over it. I thought and thought about it. And then as will sometimes happen, the meaning of the chaotic desk scene popped back into my consciousness.

"Ah yes! One of the sources of fear around speaking is not feeling prepared!"

Everyone burst out laughing. Afterward, the event planner told me that was her favorite moment of the talk. She ended up hiring me as her coach, which goes to show you that sometimes there is money in the mistakes we make. It's a service to your audience to let your blunders go.

Prepare to Change Your Mind

Every other talk I give, someone shares how frightened they are to be on a panel or to have to answer questions after they present. What happens if they don't know the answer?

You know now where this comes from. Just think of all the hours you've spent worried that you had the wrong answer, day after day, year after year. You also know how to resolve this worry. But let's look at it from a cognitive perspective.

Tell me this. Would you consider your car mechanic an expert? Presumably, yes. Do you think he or she has all the answers? Presumably not. How would you want them to handle a question you ask when they don't know the answer? Make something up to cover up that they don't know, or say, "I don't know the answer to that"?

Now, I won't pretend that I've never tried to cover up not knowing something. I mean, I went to school like most everyone. If I didn't know the answer, I fudged it, made something up. That was the name of the game.

Let me assure you, though: except in a few cases, you aren't required to be an encyclopedia. First of all, we have Google and online research. Second, no expert has all the answers, and frankly, it's just impossible to. An expert will often be the first to say that the more you know, the more you don't know. Once I realized that I didn't have to know everything, life became much easier.

Here's what I suggest you do when you don't know the answer to something:

- Say simply, "I don't know the answer to that, but I'll look it up now and let you know."

- Act like the facilitator. Say, "I don't know the answer to that. Is there anyone here who has an idea?"

- Say, "I don't know about that, but what I do know is this..." This is a good turnaround I learned from my friend, media mentor and longtime TV producer Paula Rizzo.

The thing is, even experts have their own knowledge base. Put three experts together on a panel and they are likely to disagree on something because they have their own perspective. That's fine, even good. So, relax. You don't know as much now as you will later. That's another given. You'll always be growing and learning and adjusting.

Steve Solomon is the author of many farming books and a spokesperson for the virtues of composting. Fifty percent of his family's diet came from what they grew on their homestead in Oregon. When his family's health deteriorated, he sold his farm and organic seed catalog business and they moved to Fiji.

In a matter of months, they all felt better. He could only imagine it had something to do with the food they ate and how it was grown. When he investigated the food production in Fiji, he learned that the volcanic soils were so highly mineralized that no extra fertilizer or amendment was used on the soil.

He then realized that the rain in the Northwest United States leached out some of the minerals in the soil, resulting in a mineral imbalance in both the soil and the plants grown in it. And since Solomon composted only with disposed plant material, the nutrients became exponentially imbalanced in his Oregon soil year by year, and this was the source of his family's decline in health. His whole system of thinking was turned upside down and he had to revamp his entire message.

I'm not saying that you will someday have to do an about-face in your message, but surely your knowledge and thinking about your topic will continue to evolve. So expect that and embrace the likelihood that your message will change.

Here's a similar concern: What if someone challenges you in public or asks a hard question? Novelist Jenna Blum promotes her books by giving hundreds of readings. She's had to field all kinds of questions. Here's her suggestion for dealing with the hard ones: Think about the questions you are most worried about being asked. What would those questions or challenges be? And how would you answer them truthfully? Being honest can go a long way, she states. You can say, "I was worried someone would ask that, because I know this is controversial. However, it's been my experience that [fill in the blank], and I wanted to bring it into the conversation. Thank you."

Dangers in the Real World

What about the haters? When I was streaming daily on Periscope, it was a given that trolls would come on and make nasty or inappropriate comments. We Periscopers learned how to block them without interruption. It was helpful to know that it happened to most everyone at some point and to have a simple process to deal with it.

I tell my video clients and students that the first concern is getting people to watch at all! Later, when you have more visibility, you may get folks who seem to have nothing better to do than spread their negativity. Most online platforms allow for blocking or deleting. Sometimes you may want to take a different approach and engage with them. In his book *Known*, Mark Schaefer suggests you could say, "Thank you for your dissenting view. I appreciate that you took the time to express an opinion." To learn more about dealing with haters, check out Jay Baer's popular book *Hug Your Haters*.

Serve the Audience

Before I overcame my fear of speaking, telling myself "it's not about me, it's about the audience" seemed like good advice and I said these words to myself often. At that time, though, I had to convince myself of this truth, because in my nervousness, it sure as hell felt like it was all about me. When you are in a place of fear, so much of your mental bandwidth is spent managing the fear. It's hard to fully appreciate that everyone in the audience is concerned about themselves first and foremost, and about what they can get from listening to you.

Ironically, when you take time to take care of yourself first, you can more easily focus on others. When the fear is gone, you truly can ask, *What does my audience need from me? How can I show up for them? What will make the experience better for them? How can I simplify my message so that they feel understood and inspired? How can I make it more fun for everyone?* If you've come across this idea before, consider how you can experience it in a new way.

Affirmations

Affirmations are powerful reminders to yourself of the resources you possess. At their best, they can shift your energy and put you into a mental state of confidence. As with any tool, affirmations need to be used with awareness and skill. In order for an affirmation to be meaningful, the words have to align with your current beliefs. If you feel that you are pushing the words away or not letting them in, then it's too far off point.

For instance, let's say that you always freeze up in a group when someone asks your opinion. You try out affirmations and say to yourself, "I'm relaxed, comfortable, and articulate when I speak up in a group," but it's not moving the needle for you. Yes, that's how you ultimately want to feel, but when it's too far off from what you currently believe and what your body believes, you won't get the positive shift you're looking for.

Let's say, however, that you are comfortable speaking one-on-one. You might find it more effective to say something along the lines of, "I'm relaxed, comfortable, and articulate when I speak to one person at a time, and curious to see how I can do that with two." Saying such a statement will resonate with you and bring you into an open state.

Here are some affirmations for speaking confidence. Play around with them to make them your own. Write them in a journal where you can access them easily, add to them, and update them as needed.

- I have something of value to offer, and I give it with my heartfelt love.

- I'm ready to step into a whole new level of confidence, excitement, and joy.

- I'm at ease in my brain and body; I'm relaxed, present, and focused.

- When I look at the lens, I feel kindness and curiosity toward the people that I imagine are on the other side. I feel happy and comfortable to be there.

- I feel more and more enjoyment in finding my artful articulation when I speak.

- I allow myself to not be perfect and make mistakes, forgiving myself quickly.

- When I feel resistance or a stop inside, I compassionately listen for what needs attention. What needs to be healed. And I lovingly create the space for that to happen.

- I hold in my awareness the people who are eagerly waiting for the information I have to share.

- I am full of love and appreciation for getting the opportunity to have this experience of speaking and standing in the limelight.

Gratitude and Appreciation

I want to elaborate on this last affirmation: "I am full of love and appreciation for getting the opportunity to have this experience of speaking and standing in the limelight."

Giving thanks is one of the quickest and most effective ways to shift your attitude. And it can help keep you in a more expansive mindset when it comes to speaking. Studies say that gratitude activates dopamine and serotonin. It can change your outlook from one of drudgery to one of love.

Maybe you already make gratitude a daily practice. I spend a few minutes in the morning listing things I'm grateful for: hot running water, a roof over my head, electricity, clothes in the closet, food in the fridge. And just after that list of five or ten, I can feel a definite shift inside that combines melting and tingling, and I can feel a smile spread across my face.

When you spend time in appreciation around your speaking opportunities, you trade the feeling of "I have to do this," which hides a hair of dread, to "I get to do this. How amazing," which allows you to see a much bigger picture and your place in it. What are some words of gratitude you could list?

I'm grateful for this opportunity to share my ideas; for this challenge to grow in my skills, to express my leadership, to connect with this group of people; for this chance to experiment and see what happens.

Wonderment

Wonderment is another energy shifter. It expands your worldview with your curiosity. Think about how we are on earth in these amazing bodies, as you did in the chapter on healing your self-image. What are these bodies, anyway? How is it we move? How is it that we can make sounds and talk, that you can listen to me and understand meaning from these combinations of different sounds? You can play around with this idea when you present. Think about the serendipity of people arriving at this place together, the journey of each person who comes to intersect with others for a time. Think about the amazing technology that exists so that we can communicate in myriad ways. Wonderment shifts me into a higher state of being. If this resonates with you, use it.

Expand Your Comfort Zone

I am a creature of comfort, and I love my comfort zone. Inside this well-experienced comfy space, I'm free to be me. I can play, explore, and expand my capabilities. When I hear statements such as "the magic happens outside your comfort zone" or "in order to grow, you have to leave your comfort zone," I rebel. It's not that I don't enjoy novelty and new experiences. I don't believe I have to leave my comfort zone in order to do new things. Or rather, my comfort zone includes doing new things. When you clear the fear of being seen and heard, when you lose the inner critical voice, when you free yourself of rules of behavior that someone else has imposed on you, when you align your beliefs with how you take action, you'll find yourself in a much larger comfort zone.

Your comfort zone can be a place where you can step into challenges with openness and curiosity. It's an attitude of experimentation that says, "Let's see what this is like." You find yourself in a place where trying things that are new feels good and fun.

Inevitably, you'll have new opportunities that come your way that are outside your sphere of familiarity. You'll get a call from your local media or receive an invitation for a venue well beyond your previous experience. So how do you step into new situations or environments and bring your comfort zone with you? Use the mental rehearsal technique that you learned in chapter 2. You can also use what I call the "eye-align" technique to entrain or adapt yourself to a new environment. Here's how you do it.

First, find an image that depicts your new environment or audience similar to the one you are planning for. Maybe it's a picture of a group of execs, a team around a table or a TV studio. What you can't find as an image you are likely to find in a video. Let's say you're watching a TED talk or some other performance and there is a camera shot of the audience. It might be a one-hundred-person room, a theater with two balconies, or a sports stadium with thousands. Pause the video right there.

Next, with the video frame or photo up on the screen, take a few minutes to gaze around with curiosity and relax your body. Look at details of the space, the colors and decor. Look at the people. Observe their faces and body language. All the while, pay attention to maintaining ease and calm in your body. Imagine you are aligning your energy with this environment, becoming familiar with it and building a relationship to it. That's it. Later on, you might come back and imagine giving a presentation to these audiences. For now, just "eye-align."

Know that your comfort zone isn't a fixed line in the sand. It's expandable. You can play on the edge and nudge it further out.

Exposure therapy, a form of cognitive behavior therapy, is a process for reducing fear and anxiety responses. In this therapy, a person is gradually exposed to a feared situation or object and learns to become less sensitive over time. Dr. Lars-Göran Öst, a clinical researcher and CBT founder in

Sweden, developed and popularized a single three-hour process to help an individual get over the fear of snakes. He began the treatment by speaking about the snake with the patient and moved to looking at a snake from a distance. Gradually, he took the patient closer and closer, until the person was actually touching and holding a snake without fear.

As a beginning speaker, I imagined that I would go from zero to conference stage in one step. This happens on occasion. When Moroccan Magic lip balm began to gain popularity, CEO and founder Kristina Tsipouras found herself suddenly in the limelight, asked to give talks at conferences and appear on TV. Paula Conway, founder of Astonish Media Group, similarly got tapped to speak at a General Electric event without having given a single speech in her life.

Most people follow a different trajectory, starting off small and getting larger. This approach will ease you into a larger comfort zone.

If your goal is to give talks to audiences, you might begin with a dinner at your home for friends; you can give them guidelines to jot down whatever you said that spoke to them or felt strong. Then you might speak at local libraries and rotary clubs. Next, you might add business chamber groups, associations, college clubs, and then, yes, conferences. Do as many as you can to build up your sense of familiarity.

If your speaking gigs are within a company, you might begin with speaking up at meetings and then offering to present. From there you might volunteer to be a spokesperson interdepartmentally or to speak at conferences on the company's behalf.

If you want to increase your visibility online, begin with a supportive space to learn and explore until you feel confident putting yourself in front of the public. These days, there are a multitude of online platforms. Some find livestreaming an easy first step for their public appearance because people expect livestreams to be casual and unpolished. Other people prefer to have the control of prerecorded video, so they can do multiple takes until they are satisfied.

Online Speaking: Podcasts and Webinars

To my mind, podcasts and webinars are a speaker's best friend. They allow you to focus on what you want to say without having to consider how you look. Yes, some podcasts use video and some webinars have a small circle in the corner showing your face. But for the most part, you are free from being seen.

A webinar can be an ideal first step for a speaker. You have a chance to get your material super-organized. You can even read your script! If you do read, first practice how to read without sounding like you're reading. To help you with this, check out the tools in chapter 11, "The Breath You Take and Sounds You Make."

Whenever someone reached out to be on my TV show, *Women Inspired*, I'd ask them about their podcast experience. If they had none, I recommended they aim to be a guest on four to six different ones and then circle back to me. Podcasts are wonderful because they are plentiful, conversational, and you can try out delivering your ideas in different ways each time you're interviewed. If you are working on a speech, you can plan your podcast talking points around sections of your talk.

Don't assume that if people can't see you, though, that you don't have to pay attention to your expressivity. It's even more important when people can't see you. They don't have the benefit of your gestures, facial expressions, and body language to lend nuance to your words. They have to rely on the sound of your voice in addition to your content to keep them engaged.

Consider amplifying your expressivity by 5 percent when you are voice only. It doesn't have to be over-the-top. Listen to yourself and bring variety to your tone and melody. Let yourself get excited and enthused. Remember to smile. Yes, a smile can be heard in your voice.

START WITH THIS

What permissions can you give yourself as you move forward into more visibility? Make a list of what you will allow yourself to do or to let go of in order to feel freer and more at ease.

10

Practice Your
Confident Presence

"Sunflower, open, underneath you have only begun.
Yellow and bright, you are among so many
like flowers in sun. So, stand tall."
SAM ARTHEN-LONG

Wᴇ ʟᴏᴏᴋ ᴀᴛ experienced speakers and marvel at
their sense of authority and powerful presence. They
seem so grounded and confident. They connect and
interact with the audience. It would be easy to assume that
presence and confidence come after years of experience.
After all, after years of experience, you know your material
inside and out. You've practiced speaking to different kinds
of groups in different venues. You've survived disasters and
learned how to handle the unexpected.

Certainly, experience leads to expertise. But as we
learned in chapter 1, confidence is not a guarantee. Even
seasoned speakers can lack confidence. Singer Barbra Strei-
sand famously left the stage for twenty-seven years, long

after reaching star status, not because of lack of experience or expertise—she clearly claimed both of those. No, it was from a lack of confidence.

Conversely, and importantly, a confident presence needn't be reserved only for those with years of experience and a certain number of presentations. Confidence is not a badge you receive after completing a set of tasks. You don't have to have years of experience or be "a natural" in order to build a powerful presence. You can build it right now so that anywhere you are in your speaking journey, you can take your confident presence with you wherever you go.

The problem is, too often, a confident presence is addressed as an afterthought. All of the other elements of speaking get first priority. Think about it. Generally, when you have a presentation to do, you first decide what you're going to say. You organize your content and create a script. You memorize, or prepare notes.

Suddenly when you are standing in front of people or making a video, it hits you that you want to show or present yourself in a certain light, as an authority. You become aware of your presence. Now, on top of what you want to say, new commands fire off in your brain. "Look into the lens, look into people's eyes, don't pace, don't ramble, show confidence, you just said 'um' three times!" Remember, the brain can hang on to only so many things in its consciousness at once. Your brain is now in a tangle as you try to juggle it all. That's stressful.

Yes, it can take years to develop a confident presence if the only time you practice presence is when you present. Because you afford only a slice of your attention to your presence while speaking, you develop it little by little over a long time.

However, when you remove all the distractions, you can put your full attention on what makes up confidence—you put yourself in the speed lane. Let's see how you can accelerate the process of stepping into your confidence by looking under the hood at what confidence is made of.

Explore Confidence

Merriam-Webster defines presence as "the condition of being present" and "a noteworthy quality of poise and effectiveness." Poise is further defined as an "easy self-possessed assurance of manner."

I was curious about the word "poise" and looked into the etymology. Poise is the Middle English word for "weight" or "heaviness," perhaps what in modern-day vernacular we'd call "grounded." It strikes me that the foundation of presence is an interweaving of these qualities—of being in the here and now, of ease, calm, and assured confidence, while being grounded in your body.

This definition aligns with the results of a survey I conducted of entrepreneurs and business professionals on what confidence felt like to them. Most of the descriptions that came back contained the words "centered, calm, relaxed, breathing easy."

Suzuki music teachers underscore the importance of poise and presence and take care to instill these habits from the earliest moments of learning a string instrument. When those little three-year-olds get their first cardboard violins and bows, they practice standing with their instrument and bow with poise, first under their arm and then under their chin. They practice moving it from one to the other. This careful relationship with the violin sets them up for a gracious presence as they continue to learn and grow on their instrument.

In his book *The Perfect Wrong Note*, William Westney argues that there is nothing too small to practice. He was talking about learning music, but it applies to speaking too! I love this approach because it makes learning and repatterning so much easier.

When you address various elements of presence one at a time, you have the opportunity to sink into each one and make it so familiar that it becomes automatic in the best of ways. These next chapters will be about breaking down elements of how you experience yourself on the inside so you can delight in the limelight.

Just as you might practice the delivery of content for a talk or video, or an interview—which we'll look at later—if you want to feel relaxed, you practice relaxation. If you want to feel confident, practice confidence. If you want to feel ease and flow, practice ease and flow. And when you want more presence, practice presence.

When you have only one thing to focus on at a time, practicing becomes easy, doable, joyful, and fun. As each element becomes repatterned and imprinted into your neurophysiology, you can layer on more elements. You'll be able to carry that relaxation, ease, and presence with you into new situations and environments. Your state of presence will become so familiar that it will be second nature.

Caution

These ideas I'm going to share with you about relaxation, ease, and presence are both simple and profound. Have no illusion about their place and purpose. Without doing the clearing work in previous chapters, don't expect these techniques to be the answer to your nervousness.

If you are having to push through fear, these practices can help you calm your nerves, but it's only a stopgap measure for managing fear. During my eleven weeks on daily Periscope broadcasts, these practices helped me get through the livestream, but it didn't get rid of the fear. The fear was waiting for me, needing to be dealt with each day. If you have cleared the fear and beliefs, and transformed your negative thought patterns, then there is no hump to get over or resistance to push through. You won't need to suppress or manage anxiety at the same time as you shift into a place of relaxation, ease, confidence, and presence.

Your Embodied Presence

Meditation is different from relaxation in that you are noticing what *is* rather than looking to release tension. I used to meditate in my twenties and do now as well. But there was a long period in between when meditation fell by the wayside and out of my reach—when I became a parent.

From the time my daughter was walking, she followed me everywhere I went. If I got up from the floor to go to the bathroom, it was, "Mommy, where are you going?" She was totally adorable, but I didn't have even two minutes to myself, much less thirty to quietly close my eyes. If my daughter was napping, I either napped alongside her or took advantage of the free moments to get stuff done.

However, it was during these early years of parenting that I learned I didn't have to "sit" in order to bring myself into the present. I could "be" in the midst of doing. Two of Eckhart Tolle's books, *A New Earth* and *The Power of Now*, showed me how to practice present-moment awareness when alone time was nonexistent. And as it turns out, this practice of awareness is even more transferable and relevant to you as a speaker than meditation, because speaking is active!

You can practice present-moment awareness right now as you are reading this book. While you read, ask yourself what signs of aliveness do you sense inside? Your breath? Random whirls of sensation? Do you feel cold or warm? What do you sense against your skin? Notice the position of your body. Where are your feet? How does your breath move your body?

Presence is being in the here and now. The here and now, however, is not static. It's always on the move. As you speak, you may be present and focused, but then there is a distraction, a flashing reflection in someone's glasses, the sound of a dog barking out the window. You bring yourself back. Then someone comes into the room or gets up to leave. The next words you were going to say slip away. With embodied presence, you pause and bring yourself back. With embodied presence, you continuously readjust in time. You let go of the moments as they pass by so you can move forward. You stay anchored with yourself as you move through time.

It's one thing to practice squirreled away in your own space. The real magic, though, happens when you practice in the presence of others. When you are able to stay in your body in the presence of others. I call this Embodied Connection. Let's see how it works.

Melanie stands with her eyes closed in front of the group of workshop participants. "Okay," she says. "I'm going to close my eyes and connect with myself. I feel my chest rising and falling as the air flows in and out of my nose. I feel some chilliness on my skin."

The prompt I gave Melanie was to connect with herself in whatever way that meant to her, and she was to narrate her experience. She pauses for a moment, and we hold the space as she "looks around" inside herself for sensations that pop into her awareness.

"I feel my feet on the floor," she continues. "I feel my arms resting at my side. My breath is slow. Okay, I feel connected now. I'm going to open my eyes. Thanks for letting me connect to myself in your presence."

This may be one of my favorite practices of all time— watching people close their eyes, pay close attention to the inner sensations, narrate their inner process, *and* let themselves be seen.

Narration is a key ingredient here. The narration keeps your mind focused on your kinesthetic awareness in your body that anchors you in the here and now. Imagine that!

When you do this exercise with people watching, the narration also serves to invite the audience into the experience. As we listen to you report on where your mind is focused, we follow along. When you connect within yourself, we consciously or unconsciously connect within ourselves as well. If you say you feel your feet on the floor, those of us listening will automatically feel our own feet and their relationship to the floor. If you visibly sigh and relax your shoulders, many of us do that too. This kind of mirroring has long been a central principle in dance/movement therapy but became popular when a team of neuroscientists in Parma, Italy, discovered that the brains in macaque monkeys fired off in the identical pattern whether a monkey cracked open a peanut himself or saw or even just heard another monkey do the same. In other words, the mirror neurons in our brains respond to the actions of others, the sounds we hear, and, I would guess too, the words we read.

When it comes to Embodied Connection, know that as you anchor and connect to yourself in your body, it's an invitation for others to do the same. As you do it for yourself, know that it also benefits your audience.

Now that you have a sense of how to anchor yourself in your body with your eyes closed, you're ready to try it with your eyes open.

Visual Awareness and Connection

Mandy and Sue stood facing each other, giggling.

Mandy said, "This is awkward," and the two of them erupted in a new peal of laughter. In this workshop, the exercise was to gaze into each other's eyes.

For many of us, making and keeping eye contact is highly uncomfortable. Depending on your culture, eye contact may also have rules and assigned meaning. Perhaps you learned not to look in the eyes of people of authority. Or maybe you discovered that avoiding eye contact protected your energy or kept you safe from unwanted attention.

A powerful presence, however, is not defensive; it's open and vulnerable, strong and expansive. It gives you a feeling of authority, which can be felt by others.

If I ask my students how to connect with an audience, the first thing they suggest is to look people in the eye. Ah, but if gazing into people's eyes is uncomfortable for you on its own, it's not going to suddenly feel easy and natural to do when you are giving a talk. With the premise that nothing is too small to practice, let's look at how to practice eye gazing.

You can stealth practice with the people you interact with in your life. Explore consciously looking into their eyes while you allow your body to relax. Or invite them to explore eye gazing with you in silence or while narrating your experience back and forth. Or start with a photo. Choose one that makes you feel as if the person is looking at you. It could be someone you know or a stranger who has a friendly, warm expression. Look into their eyes. Let your mind be clear of thoughts as you relax. Your eyes will naturally move around a bit and blink. That's okay. Let them. Let your eyes be nourished by what you see.

Note that the reason you feel as though the person in the photo is looking at you is that they are looking into the camera lens. They are letting their eyes be seen. This is a unique feature of the camera. When you speak live to a group of people, you can look at only one person at a time. On camera, however, there can be thousands of people watching, and if you are looking into the lens, each person can feel you are speaking right to them and that you're not just looking at them but into their eyes. That, my friend, is magic. And only on camera. And now this amazing technology is ubiquitously attached to all of our computers and devices.

If eye gazing in person feels awkward, though, gazing at the lens can be even more so. How does one relate to this technology of plastic, glass, and electricity? In the old days, the camera lens was large and easy to see. Just a glance in the right direction and your eyes were captured on the film. Nowadays, your personal camera lens is so small that it's hardly visible. A light might go on to signal "over here," but on which side of the light should you look? On some phones, there can be several lookalike dots, and you may not be sure which one is the lens for the front of the camera and the lens for the back.

Whatever device you are on, take the time to figure it out so you are sure to be looking in the right spot. With the camera on and in selfie mode, touch or almost touch where you assume the lens to be. If you have the correct spot, your finger will cover up your entire image. Be able to say for sure, "There! That's where the lens is exactly." If you use the camera on different devices, repeat this action whenever you switch. One of my clients put sticky notes with arrows on her computer camera to remind her where to look. You can do this too.

Now that you know how to be 100 percent sure of where your lens is, let's turn our attention to how to relate to it, because, let's face it, it's not natural. When you speak to that tiny dot, you can't see who is on the other side. It requires imagination. You must call up the feeling of looking at someone and recreate it. Picture someone special to you, a friend, a family member, a favorite client. Some people will stick a photo of a friendly face near the lens. With a posted photo or not, imagine you are looking at this person and smiling. Feel your body relax.

Here you are in Embodied Connection with your eyes open. You are grounded and centered in your body and connected with the person behind the lens. It's as if you are saying, *I see you and appreciate you. I can feel you here with me.*

Go one step further and feel their positive regard for you. Open yourself to receive. Remember receiving compliments? This is where you use that. Let yourself bask in their positivity. And then take that positivity and send it back to them with your gratitude for this positive regard.

The energy between you and the people on the other side of the lens flows in a circular fashion. This works just as well live, in person.

When you assume a friendly audience, you can relax in the connection. Practice this until it becomes comfortable and automatic. The lens itself can be a loving presence and you can ingrain this habit so that every time you turn on the camera, you feel yourself in a happy place.

How do you relate to the camera lens when there are others online with you, say, in an interview or online meeting? Suddenly, you have someone to look at on the screen. But should you? Unfortunately, the technology doesn't allow you to look at one another eye to eye, as you can in person. In 2020, when *everyone* was online, talk show host Trevor Noah interviewed comedian Jon Stewart. Trevor started out with some instruction. "Do me a favor and look at the lens and not the screen." Jon shook his head and said that he had been doing press conferences every day for a week and this was the first time someone had the kindness to say, "You might want to look at the camera."

I'll say this to you too. If you are in an interview and it's your turn to speak, keep your awareness of the camera as the place where you connect, just as you've been practicing. This is not to say you can't ever look elsewhere. It's natural to look around when we speak. But come back to the lens as your anchor. This decision to look at the lens is not so clear-cut, though, when it comes to online meetings where the recording isn't going to be shared to a public audience. We want to see one another. It's totally counterintuitive to not look at the person we are speaking to. I encourage you to make your own decision here. You know that if you look at the lens, others will feel you are looking at them and that will create a feeling of intimacy. Decide if it's more important for you to look at the faces on the screen or for those faces to feel your attention to them through your eyes.

Relaxation 101

Here's an obnoxious brag: I'm so lucky to own a hammock—two, actually. I hang them in the screened-in porch for the summer months. It's in those hammocks that I do a lot of my research on relaxation. As the hammock gently swings, I let my body melt into gravity. I let all my thoughts, all that stuff in my head, to drop away. I hear the whisper of the wind and birdsong and feel my breath slow down. With every breath, my body drinks in the stillness. It feels so amazing! I love hammocks!

I was not always a natural at relaxation. Quite the opposite. I had no inkling of relaxation even being a thing, let alone how to go about it. Back at age eighteen, I attended a summerlong dance therapy program with Norma Canner, a pioneer in dance movement therapy. In one of the exercises, I was instructed to relax completely and let my partner gently lift and move my arm without my control. I lay down on the floor. My partner took hold of my wrist and lifted my arm. I stiffly held my arm straight.

"Let me do it," she said.

What did she mean? I couldn't figure out what I was supposed to do. She let go of my hand and there my arm stayed stiff, pointing up to the ceiling.

She called over to Norma. "I can't get Linda to relax her arm!"

Norma came over with a kind smile. She spoke to me in a soft voice, cradled my arm in her supportive hands, gave my fingers a good shake to get my arm to drop. But I couldn't give my arm over to her. I couldn't let go of control. I failed at relaxing!

As I said, I didn't know muscle relaxation could be practiced or explored and was never taught to soften my muscles. Quite the opposite. I was taught from a young age in ballet that holding your belly and buttocks tight was a thing of beauty.

My first ballet teacher, Mr. Fokine, kept a pin in his pocket. As we girls did our pliés and relevés, if he spotted a slack gluteus maximus (Latin for butt muscle), he'd give a quick jab. That got the muscle tightened up! This is to say that even after you do the emotional and mental work of releasing and letting go, you may still need to undo the physical tension that your body acquired from whatever shenanigans happened in your life. Layer by layer, bit by bit, we coax away the tension to rediscover the mental and physical ease that lies within.

Here's why it's important. Tension in your body sends a signal to your brain that you're stressed. Your brain responds with cortisol and soon you are even more stressed. When you take time to release the unneeded muscle tension in your body, you get another bonus: your brain releases feel-good chemicals like oxytocin.

Even though you most likely will never, ever lie down on the stage when you present, I suggest you first practice deep, complete relaxation in this way—lying down on the floor or in your bed, or sitting comfortably in your chair. Stillness minimizes the stimulation coming at you, which allows you to focus your attention on what things feel like inside. Without much stimulation coming at you, you can detect subtle sensations—where you feel a sense of softness and where you are holding. You can take note of those places of tension and invite them to release and surrender to gravity.

Start by relaxing your head and face and work your way down to your toes. Go body part by body part. With your mind's eye, go inside your head, your eyes, nose, and mouth, your jaw, neck, shoulders. Imagine relaxing each organ of your body. Add more detail as it feels pleasurable.

Occasionally, I have a student who says, "I can't sit or lie still unless I'm sleeping." I get it. Really. Some people find sitting at the beach and staring at the waves their personal definition of hell. They have to be active and doing. That's why in yoga, you do active postures first before lying in meditation. It's easier to be still when your body craves it.

Sometimes the sensation of tension is simply hard to detect. Sometimes you are confused as to how to just "let go." You can create that natural desire in your body to let go if you first tense a part of your body and hold it tight. After a moment or two, let it go. You might know this practice as "progressive relaxation." When you amplify the tension in your body first, it creates a stark contrast to release and gives you a clearer place to release from.

You can also invite relaxation and ease while in motion. I will often "dance" into relaxation and ease when I want to shift into that state of being. Put on some slow music you love and give yourself a few minutes to move and breathe or gently stretch your body, all the while thinking, "relax... relax," or "ease... ease."

If you feel really hyped up and jittery, you can bounce your knees and let your upper body jiggle, jiggle, jiggle like a rag doll. Shake your hands, your arms, your shoulders, your butt, your entire body. This vigorous movement works because when you shake, you override the control of those body parts, and muscular tension can let go.

Or, in contrast, you can make your movements so micro that no one would actually notice that you are moving. Try it right now as you are reading. If you are seated, push gently down on your hips and allow your chest to rise and fall in response to your breath. Let your torso imperceptibly circle or undulate. Imagine that there is fluid in all your joints (there is) that allows your body to move without any friction. Let the micro movements open the joints in your hips, shoulders, and spine. Your mind will "read" this somatic movement as openness and flow.

If you don't know what it is like to relax when you are kicking back, it's less likely you can do it when you are standing in front of your audience. If you are not aware of tension in your jaw, mouth, and throat when your eyes are closed, you are less likely to be able to release tension when you speak. That's why I say to explore relaxation first on its own, so you know in your bones and muscles what it feels like. When you have that down, you can take it with you.

Do you want to feel relaxed on camera? Turn on your camera and relax in front of the lens. Seriously. Turn your camera on, close your eyes, and relax in front of the lens. Just as you did when you connected with yourself earlier, say to yourself, "I breathe and relax my face. I relax my eyes, my cheeks, my lips, my jaw," and so on. Do this every day. Get so used to it that every time you turn on the camera, you shift into your relaxed body and mind.

You can also stealthily incorporate this practice of relaxation into conversations with friends and clients, or into meetings with colleagues. Nobody needs to know you are doing it! While you listen to others as they speak, let your inner eye travel down your body. Feel for what is already relaxed. Invite what tension you encounter to release and let go or at least be noticed.

This practice of inner tracking relaxation and release has the added benefit of making you a better listener. For one, it keeps your mind clear of formulating what you want to say next. It also allows you to track your reactions. If you don't agree with what someone is saying, you will notice a tightening somewhere in your body. When my students use this technique, they find they become less reactive in difficult conversations.

Relaxation is a state you cultivate. As you practice, you will catch your habitual tensions and learn to let them go. This has its own reward, but it also serves to clear the physical slate so that you can create new habits of your choosing without having to push past the old.

Ease

When we built a room over the garage, the first step was to lay boards across the rafters. Even though I had little experience with carpentry, I wanted to help our carpenter friend, Doug. He was welcoming and showed me what to do and then left me to my own devices. I tentatively tapped on the nail. The nail stayed on the surface. I looked over at my friend. He planted the nail in the wood with a good whack on one or two hits. I tensed my muscles and swung hard. I missed the nail. I swung again with force. The nail bent sideways and it took two minutes to lever it out. Looking over at Doug again, I studied his swing. He had a way of letting gravity help. His motion seemed easy. I attempted to emulate his ease and the nail went in on the first hit.

What does ease feel like to you? To me, it's comfortable and nimble. I feel able to go in any direction or activity without resistance. Mentally, ease feels like a relaxed knowing. There is no worry or anxiety; there are no disturbing mental thoughts. I feel unconcerned with judgment or outcome.

The *Merriam-Webster* dictionary states that ease is how you do something with "freedom from labor or difficulty." I would modify this to say "without extra labor," because "doing" requires some effort. Ease is where you find an optimum level of effort.

Although you won't put in the same intense effort to present to an audience as you do to hit nails, you still want to nail it. You'll need to be "on," engaged, and focused. Speaking takes energy! However, if you want to feel a sense of ease, be judicious with your energy.

Many speakers find they need recuperation time after a presentation or training. Afterward, they want to curl up in a ball at their hotel or take a day off. That seems natural and like a nice thing to do—natural because throughout the day our bodies cycle between tension and release. We work hard and then relax. You put out a big effort—an exhaustive spring cleaning, a long day at work—then kick up your feet to enjoy a cool drink.

At these times, relaxation is the delicious indulgence or reward. But if you regularly find yourself exhausted after speaking, consider that you may be holding yourself in a higher state of tension than needed.

Imagine a line graph with utter relaxation at one end and high tension and effort at the other. At the utter relaxation end, you have deep sleep, meditation, and then maybe swinging on the hammock or staring at a movie screen. At the high tension and effort end, you have kayaking Class IV rapids and triathlons. Every activity can be charted somewhere along the graph. Obviously, when you speak, you don't want to be snoozing. But neither do you want to be running a sprint. You'll want to be somewhere in between. There's a "good" tension that utilizes your muscles and efforts in a productive way—to articulate your words, express your energy and passion. So, when we speak about ease, it's not that there isn't effort, it's that there's no *undue* effort.

Exhaustion suggests that you may need to shift where you habitually are on the graph between tension and relaxation. Do you go, go, go, generating all the energy for everyone in the room? Are you pushing or forcing yourself in any way? Are you tense and tight in your body? If you answer yes to any of these questions, it's time to recalibrate and calm your system down. How great would it feel to relax and be at ease with your audience!

Regenerative Braking and Your Hidden Energy Source

Many people find it exhausting to present, even when they love speaking or being on camera. Even when they get a high from all the attention, it can feel like a huge output of energy. Afterward, they need a long nap—for several days. Yes, you get charged, but when does too much charge turn into burnout? This has always made me curious. Could the experience of being in the limelight fuel you?

My mind turns to regenerative braking in vehicles, a system that makes stepping on the brake charge the battery. In the same way, you can step on the brakes to recharge your battery. What might that look like? It looks like a pause, a moment to exhale and drink in the energy of the room.

Most people feel they can't afford this moment of receiving. They're afraid that if they take their foot off the gas pedal, they'll veer off the track or lose their momentum. Try it out for yourself. Have an intention to be nourished by the space and people around you and see how it feels.

Grounded, Solid, and Strong

I once got to walk in a wood that was thick with moss all over the ground. I took my shoes off and felt the cool, soft green carpet under my bare feet. It was foot heaven.

It's quite a feat to balance on our feet. Ask any toddler. Standing requires you to connect with the surface beneath you and find balance with the deft muscles in your toes and ankles. Unlike four-legged ruminants, none of us came into the world standing. You probably don't remember the time and effort you put into figuring it out, all the times that gravity pulled you off balance and back on the floor. But you were undeterred, and chances are, delighted too. You pushed down into the ground with your ever-strengthening muscles and found verticality. Ta-da!

I remember taking my daughter to a Gymboree class when she was five months old. There were older kids there, twice her age. I looked in amazement at these other babies sitting up on their own. Wow. And some of them crawled too. Amazing! Would she ever be able to do that?

She did, and once my daughter had mastered the art of sitting up, she sat like royalty, straight and poised. I look at photos and marvel at the natural ease of her straight spine and the glee on her face. It was as if she had figured out the key to working with gravity: to push against it and balance her body. She was connected to the earth and rose up from it.

Can you imagine yourself simply sitting or standing and that being the greatest accomplishment in the world? Take a page from your younger self and feel the wonder of working with gravity, pushing down against it. Literally feel your connection to the ground beneath you.

If you're sitting, set the intention to sit with more confidence. The intention changes your body. You straighten your spine, relax your shoulders, and balance your head over top. Put your awareness on the sturdiness of your hips and butt on the chair.

Practice amplifying your physical confidence during your daily routines. While you go on errands or walk down the street or across the parking lot to the store, stride with confidence. If it helps you, pretend you are royalty or a celebrity. This can be fun!

You can play around with somatic strength in conversation—at a meeting, during a shared meal, or on the phone. Simply invite it into your body. If you are standing, connect your awareness down into your feet and feel the sturdiness on the ground. Experiment with having your feet more widely planted or close together and see how one feels different from the other.

Look, I know that as easy as this is to do, it can be hard to change these physical habits. I've had success when I think of it as my core-strength workout without having to dedicate time or go to the gym. Fitness and confidence on the go!

Take Up Space

What does it mean to you to take up space? When you present, you take up the sound space and also the physical space. When we hide, we shrink ourselves to be less visible. When we let ourselves be seen, we literally expand in our body, perhaps open up our shoulders and stand tall. You can "own" the space with your energy.

Earlier in the chapter you read about present-moment awareness. You looked inside your body and connected with yourself. You greeted different parts of your body, and as you did so, you fully embodied yourself. You took up the space inside of you.

In this same way, you can take up space in a room or environment. Have a look around you, and in your mind, greet what you see. "Hello, lamp! Hello, table! Hello, coffee mug! Hello, computer screen! Hello, window! Hello, oak tree!" As you greet the objects around you, take a moment to anchor your connection to each one. You become aware specifically of what's around you and extend yourself to each thing you see. Your peripheral vision expands as an extension of you, and you might feel how your energy encompasses what's around you. As more space fills your awareness, you'll feel yourself taking up more space.

And when you open your senses to what is around you, you anchor yourself in the place you are in. Can you see how this can support your sense of awareness when you speak? Look around and greet each part of the room and the individuals there into your awareness. Include the walls, the ceiling, and other details. Surround the room with your attention and you'll create that connection between you and the room, between you and the others in the room.

You can take this same present-moment awareness to the camera lens, just as you did with relaxation. Turn your camera on selfie mode. Look at the lens, whether on your computer or your phone. Allow yourself to become aware of your aliveness. What do you feel in your body? What do you see around you? What do you hear? Imagine that your presence can fill the room you are in from one end to the other. By looking at one wall and then the other, on an energetic level, you take up that space.

Map Your Confidence

Kathy and I were seated next to each other with our premade lunch boxes at a summer positive psychology conference. When she heard that I helped people overcome their fear of speaking, she shared, as many people do, her own speaking challenges. She told me she was scheduled to speak on a panel that week and was worried that she wouldn't be able to express her ideas well during the Q&A because she wouldn't have the questions ahead of time. I asked about her ideas and expertise, and she happily chatted away. Here she was, completely at ease and answering my questions so very articulately to me during the meal. This mealtime conversation was a happy speaking place for her, where she was completely capable of and confident in speaking extemporaneously!

I pointed this out to her and suggested she bring her awareness to this moment to capture the sense of confidence she had right then, her fluency and ease as we spoke together. I invited her to then place this sense of herself on that panel in her imagination and to see herself speaking with this same ease and flow. A grin spread across her face as she imagined the scene.

You can do this too. Where do you already have confidence when you speak? Talking one-on-one? With certain friends and family? To a large auditorium of people? Don't laugh. Some people do feel more comfortable speaking to a room of anonymous faces than to people they know.

If no experience of confident speaking comes to mind, imagine some other area in your life where you have certainty. Maybe it's working with numbers, when cooking lasagna, skiing down a slope, or dancing in the living room.

Think about what confidence feels like to you. Capture that kinesthetic image and hang on to it for a moment. Then in your imagination, put that image of yourself on that stage, in front of the camera, in that meeting room. Remember that in your imagination, anything is possible. You can amplify and expand that confident you.

Let me summarize what we covered here. First off, nothing is too small to practice. Practice relaxation, ease, present-moment awareness, grounded strength, and taking up space. The more you ingrain these feelings and attitudes in your body, the more confident you will feel when the stakes are high. You can have a relaxed presence, easeful presence, poised presence, confident presence. People will feel that immediately; they'll feel your comfort and ease, and feel comfortable and easy around you. You will immediately be seen as more credible and expert. You'll feel that way too.

START WITH THIS

If you are seated, gently push down with your buttocks and backs of your thighs and allow your torso to rise into a place of poise. This requires activating your core muscles. Notice the feeling of solidity and strength and how it shifts your mentality. Bring this stealth practice with you the next time you are in a meeting online or in person, or even just while sitting at your desk. Explore the balance of confidence and ease.

11

The Breath You Take and Sounds You Make

"As long as we are emotionally protective,
our breathing cannot be free."
KRISTIN LINKLATER

REATHING EASY: IT'S the epitome of feeling at ease, at home, and at peace with wherever you are, whether it's hanging in the hammock, hanging out with friends, or hanging with your audience.

Achieving this easy breathing asks that you bring your awareness and curiosity to your breathing experience. Respiration happens automatically, so even if you never think about it, you will still breathe. *How* you breathe, though, impacts how you feel, just as how you feel impacts the way you breathe.

Along with the fear of speaking is a certain way of breathing, usually hyperventilation. That's because when you are afraid, your body becomes tense, particularly in your belly and rib cage. With the tightness around your diaphragm, your body goes to where it can still move, the upper chest.

This is what happens with shallow breathing or hyperventilation—you bypass the diaphragm and contract the upper rib muscles to draw in breath.

If you try this, you'll get dizzy or feel breathless, as if you just ran up three flights of stairs. The fast, high breathing of hyperventilation also eliminates too much carbon dioxide, with deleterious results. Without enough CO_2 in your system, the oxygen doesn't want to leave the hemoglobin in your blood to enter your cells. This creates two problems for you as a speaker: 1) your cells don't get the oxygen they need, and 2) the lowered levels of carbon dioxide reduce the blood flow to your brain.

This means your brain is getting less blood and the blood that does get there isn't supplying your brain cells with the oxygen they need. Have a look at some of the symptoms of hyperventilation and low levels of CO_2 to see why it's to your advantage to repattern your breathing habits:

• Impaired concentration
• Poor memory
• Unreality
• Rapid heartbeat
• Dizziness
• Trembling hands

The movement of your breath shows up differently depending on what else you are doing with your body. When your belly muscles are relaxed, you'll see minimal chest expansion; rather, the movement will be lower down in your belly.

It's not just stage fright that disrupts our breath. It's the accumulation of stress that builds up each day, and over weeks and months. It's the constancy of commitments, concern about world events, the relentless to-do list. You may walk around with a knot in your belly and a band around your ribs.

Because how you breathe is habitual, any anxious patterns you've built up over time are not going to automatically and fully clear away as you resolve your past issues. Muscle tension has its own allure called muscle memory. Because of this muscle memory, it will take some focused attention and intention to find a new groove with your breath.

Let's break it down so you can create a new pattern of efficiency and ease. At its most basic, breathing goes like this: inhale, exchange oxygen with carbon dioxide (CO_2), exhale. Next, we have the diaphragm. This muscle lives tucked up inside your rib cage just below your heart. When the diaphragm receives a brain signal that the CO_2 level in your blood is rising, it contracts, flattens down, and pushes your organs downward into your belly.

If your abdominal muscles are relaxed, your belly will balloon out to make room for the expanding lungs. This is what is meant when yoga teachers suggest you "breathe into your belly." You aren't actually drawing air into your belly; rather, you're allowing the expansion of your lungs to have a ripple effect of organ displacement.

As you know and can feel in your body, the muscles around the ribs also expand out and up. The volume of space inside the lungs increases three dimensionally if your muscles are soft as the air rushes in.

Then, if you are at rest, your exhalation is a passive release. Just like an elastic band, the diaphragm and rib muscles recoil to their neutral position. The air in your lungs is expelled into the atmosphere, taking the carbon dioxide with it. The abdominal muscles that were stretched and the belly organs likewise rock back to their resting place.

Most of us aren't taught how to breathe. We just do it. But how we breathe indeed changes our life experience, our health, and our well-being.

I didn't think much about breathing until the day my sisters pinned me on the floor at our grandma Molly's apartment and tickled me mercilessly. I laughed so hard, but it wasn't happy laughter. I laughed against my will. It became too much. And then it happened: I couldn't take a breath. It got stuck. I spasmed and couldn't move. I wanted to scream, "*Stop!*" But nothing came out. Frozen in time. It felt like an eternity. I thought, *I'm going to die.*

I'm not sure how I recovered. Maybe my sisters saw my lips had turned blue, and screamed at me or hit me on my back. Maybe they pulled me up by my arms and that somehow released the spasm. It must have scared the bejeezus out of them, because even though tickling their little sister was their favorite torture of choice, they promised right then and there that they would never do it again.

The next time I remember thinking about breathing was when I began voice lessons after traveling around the world for a year. I missed music! We had no portable stereo systems back in the seventies. I promised myself that when I got back to Boston, I'd take voice lessons. I didn't know that it would involve pondering how to breathe.

It seemed that every voice teacher I studied with had their own idea of how to use the breath. One teacher suggested a long, deep breath through the nose before singing a song with a long line. Another teacher suggested minimizing the air I take in. A Balkan singing teacher said that I should pull my stomach in tight after an inhale to give power to the voice. Another said to fill my belly like a balloon, to hold it gently extended while I slowly let the air escape. I wondered, which breathing technique should I practice? What's the "right" way to breathe? One day, while hanging backward over a large blue physio ball with my hands on my lungs, I called out, "Why didn't my mother teach me how to breathe?!"

I found the situation enormously frustrating until it occurred to me how entirely flexible and nuanced our breath can be. And that there are numerous ways to engage the breath for different purposes. Our breath has the extraordinary feature of both running completely on automatic and being under our control. We use our breath to sing and shout, to grunt when we lift heavy furniture, to pump faster when we run, to hold when we dive into the lake, to sigh with relief, to calm ourselves down and bring ourselves into the present moment. This breath stuff is pretty extraordinary and throughout the ages, people have experimented with the breath to test its capabilities.

Pranayama is the Hindu word for the regulation of breath through techniques. It's as old as the practice of yoga. Other breathing practices come out of the Buddhist and other traditions, and today we continue to experiment and innovate. There's the 1:2 rule, where you breathe in a certain number of counts and breathe out for double that number—for example, you breathe in to the count of four, and then breathe out to the count of eight. There's the 4-7-8 technique, where you inhale to the count of four, hold to the count of seven, and exhale to the count of eight. These are techniques that people have made up. You can make up your own too. The most important part of any of these techniques is to notice what it does for you.

In my early years performing with the world music group Libana, I looked for practices to calm my nerves before the show. I was usually dressed and made up before the others, which left me time to compose myself. I'd sit in a corner and regulate my breath with a counting game. Measured breaths will tone your diaphragmatic muscles and snap you out of shallow hyperventilation. It gives you a feeling of control too. In fact, some call this kind of breath exercise, where you count, controlled breathing.

Gentle Breath

If counting breaths gives you control, gentle breath brings you ease. I discovered gentle breathing inadvertently, while trying to get rid of my hiccups. On this day, I had exhausted all the usual recommendations—scare myself, drink water bent over from the opposite side of the glass, stick my fingers in my ears while holding my breath. Usually, one of these would work after a try or two. But on this particular day, none of them did. My hiccups persisted.

The thought *just be still* passed through my mind. I closed my eyes, put a hand on my heart, and put my attention on stillness. I made my breath as little as possible, not to starve myself of oxygen, but to savor "just enough." I repeated the words, "Shhh, quiet, gentle, still." Within seconds, the hiccups disappeared. I waited a few moments for them to return, but they didn't.

I later taught this to my daughter, who went through a period of frequent hiccups. She'd come to me to guide her. I put a hand on her chest and whispered, "Shhh, quiet, gentle, still." Worked like a charm every time.

If you haven't already quieted your breath while reading this, take a moment to experience it now. Imagine that the air is the most delicious elixir in the world. Let your exhale be a sweet release without effort. The muscles of your diaphragm and ribs simply release and let go.

Savor the air you need. Don't be stingy and shortchange yourself. But don't overdo it, either. Find the smallest "right amount" and let your body determine what that right amount is from one breath to the next. Your body will automatically adjust from breath to breath, letting you know if it wants more or if it can do with less.

In order to be flexible and ready to respond to what amount of air your body desires, you need to remove any holding or blocks in your breathing apparatus. Imagine you can loosen up the tiny muscles that connect rib to rib, so that they expand without restriction. Soften, too, the area around your diaphragm and belly. Remember that when the diaphragm contracts and flattens out, it pushes down into the belly area and moves the organs. That's why your belly will rise when you lie on your back, relax, and breathe. It's not the actual air filling your belly but, rather, the displacement of your organs as the diaphragm pulls down.

In his book *Conscious Breathing*, Gay Hendricks offers a metaphor for removing the blocks you encounter when you breathe for ease. Imagine you want to water some plants with a garden hose, but when you turn the faucet on, no water comes out. *Oh*, you think, *there must be a kink in the hose*. When a hose is bent, the water can't flow through. You look along the length of the hose to find where it's bent. And when you unkink it—whoosh—the water flows through. Your breath is like that. Look inside your body to locate any blocks of tension and "unkink" them. Then enjoy the softness of your easy breath.

I like to play a game when I'm in a swimming pool. I inhale, dunk under the water, and let the bubbles flow out from my exhalation. After the bubbles are gone, I let my body go completely limp in silence. I pretend I'm a jellyfish, with no bones in my body, floating gently beneath the water. I pay particular attention to softening the area around my diaphragm. When I feel a gentle urge for air, I push my feet on the pale blue bottom and rise to the surface for an easy inhale, then drop back with an exhale into my jellyfish underwater float. The feeling is delicious.

It was during this play that I discovered the magical stillness after an exhale. During this long pause when the movement of the breath stops, you can feel your entire body release tension on a deep level.

Here's an opportunity for some stealth practice. You don't have to be in the water to experience the quiet and delicious deep space after the exhale. You can do it right here as you read.

Take in a lovely, feel-good amount of air and let it go. Then pause and relax as you wait for the next request to breathe. The pause may be short, or it may go on for thirty seconds or more. Don't be concerned if it goes on for quite a while. Simply continue to enjoy the melting quality of the stillness. If you focus your attention at the bottom of your rib cage and keep it completely relaxed, you'll sense the subtle reflex, that tug on your diaphragm that lets you know it's time to inhale another lovely, feel-good amount of air.

I'm spending all of this time on relaxation, ease, and breath so these qualities repattern into your neurophysiology and become second nature. This way, your breath becomes an ally you can depend on. So that when you are preparing for a presentation, you know this place of serenity in your tissues. You can call up relaxation instantly with a mere wisp of awareness, so that when you look at the people sitting before you or into the camera lens, you are anchored in your present-moment awareness. You are serene and unflappable.

Breathe to Speak

Now that you are tuned into the subtleties of the unencumbered flow of air, let's turn to how you can bring that into your speaking. Because it's your breath that powers your speech; your words ride on your breath.

Just as we are usually oblivious to how we breathe throughout our day, we are also oblivious to our breath when we speak. We just speak. That's how it should be. You want to be able to focus on communication and let everything else run on autopilot. This works as long as the automatic settings are fully functioning. Let's ensure that they are.

When I first learned to swim, I was told to hold my breath when my face was in the water. I hated the front crawl. I got so exhausted. My breath didn't function well. Later, a counselor at summer camp suggested that rather than hold my breath in the water, I blow the air out and make bubbles. She also advised that I practice the timing so that my air was comfortably used up when I lifted my head for the next inhale. So much easier!

The breath we use in the water mirrors how we breathe to speak. We take a quick inhale, and the words bubble out on the exhale. When we get to a natural pause, like a comma or a period, we let the air come in again.

The most significant difference in our breath from when we rest to when we speak is how we exhale. At rest, exhalation is a passive thing. Your diaphragm and intercostal muscles simply release and recoil back to neutral position. For speech, this quick release won't take you further than a grunt or sigh. To string words together, you need to control the outflow of air.

When you speak, the air meets resistance at the vocal folds and sets them into vibration. In order to keep the sound going with your words, you need to keep the air pressure moving through your vocal cords. You do this by using a combination of your abdominal and intercostal muscles to hold your rib cage open. This slows down the outgoing passage of air enough to get a string of words out before you take another breath. Generally, your body does a good job of parceling out your breath for speech.

However, if you aren't fully in a place of ease, tension can accumulate in your body. The more tension, the less air you take in—and the less air you have available to finish your sentences. You may notice your voice starts to sound squeaky or gravelly. Your throat might ache. Or you may find yourself (*gasp*) gasping for air!

Allocate a small part of your brain to keeping its attention on the feeling of ease in your body. As you sense you need to take another breath somewhere in a long-winded sentence, you can fit one into a logical pause instead of squeezing the last bit out. And if you get to the end of the sentence with some tension in your abdomen or unused air in your lungs, you can quickly let it go so that the breath flows in without the impediment of tight muscles. This easeful speaking on your breath results in a nimble flexibility that will allow your words to follow your feeling impulse.

In her book *Freeing the Natural Voice*, vocal coach and acting director Kristin Linklater says when you inhale from a place of relaxation, the breath becomes free to respond to your thoughts and feelings, which will be expressed through your speech.

The Sounds You Make

Singers warm up their voices in many ways that they will never use in performance, but they do it because it opens up their sound. That's what we are going to do here. Warm up the parts of your vocal anatomy for speaking so that you have a lot of range to draw from as you tell stories and make your points.

Everyone has their own habitual way of speaking. We can often recognize someone we know just by the sound of their voice. Isn't that amazing? You have a sound print that is unique to you. Or nearly. That's why it's also a surprise when we come across two people who sound somewhat alike.

It's also amazing that as infants, we have the capability to learn any language in the world. Through our particular anatomy, mimicking those around us, and, as you know now, the experiences and values that shaped your expression, you evolved the sound of your voice.

When you begin to explore with your voice, it's likely feelings will come up. You may hit against some past belief or decision you made about how you should sound. Or it will highlight a painful experience from the past. There's a good reason for this: the vagus nerve. In case you've not heard of it, the vagus nerve has important functions:

- It activates virtually all of the muscles used for sound and speech—all the muscles that open, close, tense, or relax the vocal folds, including the diaphragm.

- It mediates between your brain and your gut sensations and emotions.

This is all to say that your vocal apparatus and gut emotions are connected through the vagus nerve. It makes perfect sense that expressing yourself through speech can be a highly emotional activity. It was for me.

In my mid-twenties, I traveled solo for a year around the world. Out in the countryside in Nepal, I realized how much I missed playing my LP records, like Jefferson Airplane and Joni Mitchell, and the sound of the songs I enjoyed. I tried to make up for the lack by singing these songs myself. To my utter dismay, I discovered that without the recording, I didn't know the words to any of my favorite songs from beginning to end. I decided that when I returned to the States, I would take voice lessons and learn some songs.

I reached out to Susan Robbins, whom I had seen perform in New England just before I left on my trip. I was quite excited about my first lesson, but as soon as I opened my mouth to make a sound, tears welled up in my eyes. It was as if all of my emotions from having been shushed or silenced or hurt came rushing to the surface. I wailed through many a lesson after that. Indeed, Robbins says that this is common among her students. "At some point," she said, "their story reveals itself as they work on loosening the muscular tensions that hold back their voice."

You may be wondering why I am speaking about the emotions in the voice now, instead of in the earlier sections of the book. I could have had, for instance, a section on learning to love how you sound. I have it here instead, because it is in the doing, in the opening of your mouth to explore sounds and in the letting go of vocal tension, that these emotions appear. Stuff doesn't come up from the past in a neat order or even all at once. Something new will arise and surprise you just when you think you have it all taken care of. I want you to be ready for this. Now that you have the awareness and tools, as you uncover something new that blocks your speaking, you can address it and clear it away.

Delicious Diction, or, How to Fall in Love with Your Voice (Again)

Your speaking does not emerge disembodied. You speak with your body powered by your breath, shaped and supported by the structures in your head and torso. You may generally like your voice or not give your voice much thought until you listen to a recording of yourself speaking. Then suddenly you are weirded out. It doesn't sound like what you hear inside your head.

You're right: what you hear in your head is different from how your voice is captured on technology. Rest assured that everybody has this disconnect when they first hear their recorded voice. Over time, it will become familiar to you, just as the voice inside your body is familiar. Are you ready to love your voice? Let's go.

Warning: The exercises that follow in this chapter may draw people and animals to see what the heck is going on. You may want to give advanced warning to housemates that some weird sounds might emerge from your room.

As a child, once you mastered your ability to speak, unless you studied theater arts or singing or had a speech impediment, you rarely gave your speech production much thought again. You might notice that it's hard to speak when you're jogging with a friend or climbing flights of stairs. If you are like most people, though, your attention is on the words you want to say and not on the production of sound.

But let's imagine the young child's experience. Babies are fascinated by their ability to create sound. They spend endless amounts of time in sound play. And they derive pleasure from the experience. I invite you to return to that experience of the child in your own sound-making. When you bring your awareness to include the tangible sensations in your body, you open up the door for your sounds and words to become a physical experience.

Unless you sing much, and even if you do, the area of your vocal source can feel like a foreign country and uncharted territory. We don't know what's going on in our throat, really. We probably knew more as a two-year-old than we do now. We've forgotten. We got distracted by other things. Had other concerns. But now, you want your voice to carry authority, confidence, and meaning. Without felt awareness, we don't have much agency to make it work for us in an intentional way. In the remainder of this chapter, you'll get to zoom in to investigate your personal sound-making instrument, build upon your relationship to your vocal production, and make it work for you.

Love the Sound of Your Voice

The expression "he loves the sound of his own voice" is used as a put-down for someone who talks too much and dominates the conversation. You may have heard this and decided you weren't going to be *that* person. Yet, every child loves the sound of their voice. Sounding is a pleasure. The vibration feels good in the body. It can feel soothing, even healing. Getting to speak and be heard is both an honor and an opportunity to love and enjoy the sound of your voice. It's one of the ways you can delight in the limelight.

Don't feel as if you have to consume this vocal exploration all at once. In my programs, we take eight weeks to cover the different parts, with suggestions for daily discovery.

Let me break it down for you in a few steps so that you can experience the elemental parts of speech for yourself.

Open Resonance

You know the phrase "speak from your heart"? Why does the heart get all the attention? After all, it's the lungs that give rise to our voice, not the heart. The lungs cradle the heart and massage it with every breath. The lungs provide the bow for the violin of your vocal folds. The lungs are the source of your ability to speak with emotion and power, nuance and subtlety. Why does the heart take all the glory? It's not the heart's fault. It's ours.

The phrase could be reframed as "speak from your lungs," but it doesn't sound as good or sexy. Maybe the lungs need a new stage name. In any case, I'd like to give the lungs their due. As you move through this chapter, give your lungs their due too.

Let's focus first on the touch of air across your vocal cords—the air/vocal vibration. Awareness of this touch will bring a round, warm resonance to your speaking voice. Right now, as you read this, open your mouth, let your tongue and lips and jaw completely relax. You might have to move your jaw or tongue around a bit to find what relaxed feels like. Good. Now, when you feel the very back of your tongue is relaxed, whisper the vowel, "Ah" just on air, as if you're just exhaling it. See if you can feel what happens in your throat to produce that sound. Say it once, and then relax. After a moment, say it again. Relax in between each time to give the vocal tissues a chance to rebound. Sometimes it's in the rebound that you more easily detect the movement of your speech production.

After you try this three or four times, relax even more. I call this deeper relaxation a "full reset." When you have felt inhibited to speak in any way, that tension can also infringe upon the structures that produce sound. As you explore the sounds in the rest of this chapter, tension will regularly want to creep back into your vocal apparatus. So be sure to reset frequently and do a full reset every few minutes. Let all the tension go. If you do nothing else, look for relaxation and ease in your sounding.

Now, still with the back of your tongue and jaw relaxed, say the same vowel, "Ah," but voiced with sound. Feel how voicing the vowel is different from just letting the air out. Certainly, it sounds different. But the sensation in the throat will be different as well. Go back and forth between just the air on "ah" and then with sound vibration. Zoom in to your throat to notice the difference. Place your fingers on the front of your throat to collect more information. Where do you feel the most movement? How high up and down your throat can you detect that sound engagement? Try it out a bit louder. Where in your body can you feel vibration? On your jaw? Your sinuses? Your chest? Somewhere else?

It's tricky to find ease and relaxation when you speak because phonation, the production of sound, requires action, which is muscular effort. And there are lots of moving parts when you speak. Therefore, the goal is not to be completely and utterly relaxed when you speak. The aim is to find balance between effort and ease and to enjoy your vocal expression.

Resonance Across the Vowels

The shape you make with your tongue and mouth creates your vowel sounds. In school, we learn about the five vowels: A-E-I-O-U. However, we have many more vowel sounds in the English language. Below is a list of some one-syllable words. Notice the shapes that your tongue and mouth need to make for each vowel sound inside these words. How are they different from one another? First say the word and then just the vowel. For each vowel, connect with the resonance of your air across your vocal folds. Notice, too, if certain vowel sounds come along with tension. If so, see if you can find a new way of producing the sound without constriction. Here's the list of words: Say, see, sod, so, sue, sat, sand, sit, set, sun, saw, sir.

Let's apply this vowel resonance to the words of a sentence. We will get more into articulation of different consonants later. But I want you to get a feel for what can change even with this little bit of sound exploration.

Start to read out loud. Right here in this book. Yes, read these next few paragraphs out loud. (If you are in a public space, you get a free pass to come back and do it later.) Read the words in slow motion. Put your attention on the very back of your tongue where it meets your throat. Invite a sense of balanced ease to the back of your tongue and jaw as you shape the vowels in the words you read. Don't worry about over- or under-enunciating.

Right now, aim to find resonance on every single vowel. Remember, slow motion. Some vowels will feel naturally resonant for you. With others, you'll have to figure out how to make them so.

Speed up one notch, still with your awareness of balanced effort and ease in the movements in your tongue and jaw and the touch of breath from your lungs. Don't go for perfect. Go for interesting and fun.

Word Dance

If vowels carry the resonance in your voice, the consonants provide texture and rhythm. Consonants, by definition, interrupt or break up the continuous sound of the vowel.

The key to a round vibration in your voice is to articulate just enough consonant but then to get off it quickly to make room for the next vowel resonance.

Most everybody has a funny story of mishearing words or the lyrics of a song. Try saying these two phrases: "Kiss this guy" and "Kiss the sky." You can see why listeners to Jimi Hendrix's "Purple Haze" got confused. This was way before you could look up lyrics on the web.

If you want to be understood, you can make it easier for your listeners by learning to articulate well. This is a particular challenge for speakers for whom English is an additional language. If English is an additional language for you, this section will help you tremendously.

But it's not just for non-native speakers. It's for all speakers. And it's fun. Playing with articulation is fun. Pretend you are a child and play along. These explorations can also be converted to better learn any language.

Your tongue is a master player in the articulation of sounds. Some letters are formed with the front of the tongue, and others, with the back. Let's start in the back, since that's closest to the origination of your vowel production.

As you read out loud and follow the movements of the tongue, I suggest you slow down and say each sound multiple times. There is so much happening here. I want you to zoom in where the tongue is hitting in the back of your mouth to make these different consonant sounds. Go back and forth between different sounds to compare the action. You might find that you create the action a bit differently from word to word depending on what comes before or after.

Back of the tongue consonants. Start with the "ah" vowel, then explore with others.
kah, gah, yah, ha
Words using these consonants: go, cat, yacht, hay

Front of the tongue sounds. Feel for which structures the tongue touches to make these sounds.
tah, dah, la, the, th
Words using these consonants: tea, dough, lie, these, think

The tongue also works in tandem with the jaw. Notice what the jaw and tongue do differently to produce these sounds.
cha, juh, zuh, sah, sha, zha
Words using these consonants: chair, jug, zeal, sass, shoe, casual

As you continue to read out loud, switch your attention to the movement of your lips. Allow yourself to watch and feel with curiosity how your lips are moving forward and back and out and together to make the shape of vowels and the sounds of certain consonants. Let's break it down into smaller pieces. Imagine yourself like a baby trying on sounds and notice the amazing lip action required to create them.

buh, buh, buh
puh, puh, puh
v, v, v
f, f, f
mu, mu, mu
yo, yo, yo
you, you, you
shush, shush, shush
ruh, ruh, ruh

If you allow yourself to accentuate your lip awareness, you'll build up the muscles for better lip articulation.

Quick review: Your jaw, lips, and tongue move together in complex combinations to form the vowels and consonants while the air from your lungs vibrates your vocal folds to create the resonance in your voice.

You won't be able to feel or be aware of all the moving parts at once—at least, not right away. However, as you speak, you can move your awareness around to different moving parts. First you might put your attention on the shape of your lips and then focus for a while on the front of the tongue as it moves around the mouth. Then you might bring your attention to the back of the tongue for those throat consonants.

When practiced with mindful awareness, the movement of the mouth feels sensual. You become a master articulator of your sounds. Your diction and articulation will also become nimbler, and people will find it easy to understand each word you say. It's a win for you and a win for your audience. Add to that the resonant vibration your voice creates and speaking becomes a full-bodied pleasure.

I want you to love the sound and feeling of your voice. Literally. When you love your voice, it won't mean you'll dominate all your conversations, but it will offer you a big bonus of pleasure when it's your time to speak.

Your Dynamic Range

Back in my young adulthood, I put on several solo improv dance performances. At each performance, I included a short piece using three words. In one performance, the three words were, "I don't know." In another, they were, "I don't care."

It's amazing how many ways you can say those three words, and I had so much fun playing around with them. I now call it the "I Don't Care Game." Try it out for yourself. Say the sentence over and over, each time in a different way. Place the stress on different words one at a time. "*I* don't care. I *don't* care. I don't *care*. *I DON'T CARE!*"

Say it slowly. Say it fast. Say it with disdain, exasperation, confusion, anger, angst, pain, compassion, love, indifference. Say it as questions. Say it singingly. Play around going up or down in pitch. So many ways to play it!

You can do this same thing as you practice a script, imagine that every sentence has a shape of its own. Give every sentence its own variants. (Unless you are creating a rhythm with repetition on purpose.) Playing with a script this way is magical. It will give lots of variety and interest to your speaking.

Here are a couple more ways to bring more variety into your speaking voice and have fun:

- Read children's books out loud, changing your voice for each character. Go all out with playful voices. Find the extremes in your voice. The biggest enthusiasm, the breathiest, scariest, or twangiest voices you have.

- Imitate the voices of people you listen to online. Try to capture the nuance in the voice of the person speaking. You may not ever use a different accent in your own speaking, but this practice will widen your vocal production.

Show Up for Practice

"Linda! Your tongue!" The Nancy Drew novel fell out of my lap as I startled to attention. I noticed the thickness of my tongue between my teeth and pulled it back inside my mouth. I was twelve years old and still had my childhood "tongue thrust," as the doctor called it. My sisters called it "sucking on your tongue," which was more descriptive. Whenever I concentrated, daydreamed, or spaced out, which was often, I stuck out my tongue to suck on it, like a cute little baby. Only, at my age, this was no longer cute, but alarming. How could I go through life with my tongue hanging out of my mouth? My mom and sisters took to different strategies to get me to stop.

I have a photo of me sitting in a comfy living room armchair with curlers in my hair, laughing with all my silver braces showing. Braces because my tongue thrust had pushed my teeth out. My sisters had snuck up on me to take a Polaroid of me in the act. They hoped that showing me the photo of what I looked like might be the cure. Mission unfulfilled. I caught sight of them just before they snapped the shutter.

Mom thought speech therapy would help. Twice a week, I rode my bicycle to Mrs. Brown's house, whose daughter, Alice, was good friends with my sister. We'd spend the hour repeating different sounds of speech to get the muscles of my tongue more active and agile. She would watch me swallow water from a glass and give me tips on how to do it better.

It could be that the speech therapy and muscle training helped. All I remember is that when my braces came off at the end of the year, my tongue thrust was gone as well. Hallelujah! I was saved from a lifetime of ostracism and embarrassment. What I acquired, though, was tension in my tongue that made my throat hurt to sing, a tension that's taken a lifetime to undo.

You can train your voice in any number of ways—to be lower with roundness and resonance, to be more melodious and varied and expressive. You can train your voice to be more articulated, to be less nasal, or carry a further distance without strain. It takes patience, desire, repetition, and focused attention on technique.

You can't read this chapter without trying sounds out loud and expect to transform your voice. Your voice is a nuanced system of muscles and movement grooved into your neurophysiology. You need to explore these sound ideas over weeks and months or longer. It doesn't have to be hard, though, or complex. If you simply hum a bit in bed each morning and feel for the touch of sound across your vocal cords, you'll feel a difference in your voice. With any amount of attention, you'll make headway. The good part is that it is fun and fascinating and forgiving. Speech leaves lots of room for variance. We don't have to match pitch or rhythm, like when we sing.

In Dr. Ivan Joseph's TEDx talk on self-confidence he tells the story of a man from Colombia whom he recruited for the college soccer team. Although the player was terrific with his feet, he couldn't catch a ball. The solution was to kick the ball against the wall and catch it. His goal was to do it 350 times a day for eight months. Did he learn to catch? Yes, and he now plays soccer in Europe.

I'm not going to suggest you repeat an exercise 350 times a day for eight months. But I found it helpful to know that's what a top athlete or performer might do to create a new pattern. Know that you aren't crazy, that nothing is wrong with you if you need to or want to dedicate this kind of time.

I've been in weekly voice lessons for the past forty years (still at it) to learn to sing with a voice I love to listen to. Here's my simple takeaway that I learned from the Estill Model of voice training: go for how it feels as much as how it sounds. When your voice vibrates warmly in your chest, when you enjoy the nimble movements of your mouth as you speak, when the expression of your words add nuance to the meaning, that's when you fall in love with your speaking voice.

As you connect more tangibly to the sounds you make, more and more, you'll feel like you are speaking from deep inside—because you are. You'll feel your thoughts, your words, and your sound are all of one piece. And because of the mirror neurons inside us all, you will bring your audience to a deeper-felt somatic place in themselves too.

START WITH THIS

Stand up and have a look around your space. Greet the things you see with robust enthusiasm.

"Hello, lamp! Hello, window! Hello, tree! Hello, painting on the wall! Hello, computer!"

Keep going with these greetings for a couple of minutes. See if you can make each one unique and different in its melody and expression. Feel the resonance in your body and round smoothness in your sound. Then notice how your speaking voice has changed.

12

Expressively, Naturally You

*"Shine bright and in your light
you will wake up the world."*
GABBY BERNSTEIN

STOOD WITH TWELVE other women in a circle, our
arms wrapped around each other in a cocoon of camara-
derie. We had just spent the last four days writing, sharing
what we'd written, and basking in the positive reflections of
the group. It was one of those cozy environments, a Gateless
Writing retreat led by Suzanne Kingsbury, who had created
this space for us to fall in love with our words.

In this ending ritual to our time together, Suzanne spoke
our names one at a time and the rest of us called out words
that expressed what we saw in each person she named. It
was a time to celebrate each individual for their qualities as
we experienced them. I heard my name and the words that
followed—warm, caring, soft, radiant, encouraging, introspective, teacher.

While all of these reflections were lovely and beautiful, I
noticed in myself a yearning to hear other words alongside.

Words like "bold," "funny," "playful"—I knew those things were part of my essence too. My daughter and husband find me hysterically funny. My close friends perceive me as bold. Somehow, though, these qualities were not seen by these ladies during our week together.

It occurred to me that if I wanted to hear those words reflected back to me, I'd have to do something different. I'd have to break out of my prescribed ways of being and express those parts of myself more freely. I'd have to expand who I am and let that be seen.

How we come to express ourselves in the way we do is complex and honed over time. Part of it is shaped by some unique inner mystery that seems to emerge all on its own when you're born. You know, of course, that our expression has also been shaped by our past negative experiences. Part of it is shaped, too, by how we are praised. If people like something we do, we do more of it. If they don't like it, we might do less.

Maybe you, like me, have been praised for being under-standing, warm, a great listener, a safe companion. You like being all those things, but a hidden part of you inside yearns to also be seen as passionate, badass, or bold. Or maybe you've been told how you are the life of the party and you yearn to also be seen as thoughtful, organized, or real. Maybe you've been told, "You've always been quiet." Or maybe you feel like you used to be adventurous as a kid and somehow that characteristic got lost by the wayside.

Take a moment to think of the words your friends, family, and clients use to describe you. What words would you love to hear as well? Write them down. In this chapter, we're going to look at ways for you to both uncover more of what's inside and build upon those things with new ways of being yourself.

At the start of my coaching journey, my go-to, warm, supportive, and calm way of expressing myself was (and still
is) useful as a coach wanting to provide a safe space for my
clients. I made a lot of relaxation recordings, so my default
way of speaking is slow. If I spoke to a crowd the same way I
speak when leading a visualization or relaxation, I'll put my
audience to sleep. As a speaker, I want and need to bring out
a wider range of dynamics.

I'm not suggesting that you be inauthentic. Of course,
you want to be "naturally you." But what does that mean?
When I think about being naturally me, I get confused.
Which "me" is the natural one? Is it the "me" who quietly
observes in a group? The "me" who cracks silly jokes with
my daughter?

It's the best of ourselves in all of these places that we seek
to bring together when we are in the limelight. It's all the
things that we are yet to be.

Build Upon Who You Have Been

Think about those qualities you want to be known for and
build them into your life. Every day, play with one small
thing. If you are on a phone call or in conversation, speak
a little louder, with more enthusiasm or drama. If you are
with your closest friends or family, surprise yourself and do
something uncharacteristic but still you. Jump up and down
with excitement or skip down the street. Act something out.
Sing a line instead of saying it.

Take a class in something you haven't tried before, like
drumming or singing, or some kind of improvisation. The
beauty of improvisational forms is that your self-expression is

what it's all about. There is nothing extra to learn except the rules of the game and how to put aside your self-judgment so you can express yourself freely. Yes, the nonjudgment, again, is key.

Charles Limb studied the brains of jazz improvisers and freestyle rappers to figure out what allowed them to create so much material on the fly and so freely. It looked like the area of the prefrontal cortex that monitors impulses was deactivated. In other words, the part of the brain that worries about if something is good enough or what people will think was turned off. This meant that new ideas could be generated without inhibition.

Learning something new automatically creates new neurophysiological patterns. If you tend to be quiet and then you bang with all your strength on a drum each week, that's going to change your sense of self. If you are stiff in your body and take a salsa class that swings your hips, you are going to bring more sensuality to your movements. If you are a perfectionist and take an improv class, you will bring in more spontaneity and silliness to your life and to your speaking. The point here is to widen your scope of behavior so you have more qualities to choose from.

Move and Speak

During a Q&A on a college campus, a student asked me how to use movement and gestures to make presentations more interesting. My answer is to allow yourself to explore the connection of your words and ideas with your body. Allow your body to participate in shaping the meaning of what you say.

Think about it. Your body movement adds to and enhances the meaning of your words. You already do this to some extent. Just as everybody speaks, everybody moves. Perhaps, though, you would like to feel more comfortable in your body in more places more of the time.

To become more connected to your movement, provide some space and time to get intimately familiar with how your body already likes to move. Give your body space to speak on its own, without direction, interruption, or judgment.

My favorite way to do this is to close my eyes and let my body move how it wants. All I do is witness myself with a curious mind. You might remember my story of dancing my feelings out after school. Or the Authentic Movement I studied in grad school. It's like that. You're not telling your body to stretch or to perform in some way. Rather, you are letting your body speak to you in its native language, movement. Think movement meditation or stream-of-consciousness movement and you get the idea. Spending time this way, you'll find out what is natural to you. You'll go from self-consciousness to self-awareness.

The more you feel connected to your body, the more you will trust its movement when you speak. As you explore movement, you will feel more and more comfortable in your skin. Your movement will become familiar. You'll become aware of how standing feels different from sitting. How moving sideways feels different from walking forward or backward. You'll feel a sense of spontaneity in your movement, whether it's choreographed or improvised.

If you are drawn to the idea of using movement to expand your self-expression, you can make a special playlist to dance to that invokes and invites different qualities. Think of it like a buffet menu. Pick from serene to sultry, playful to powerful, heartful to sensual, expansive and explosive. You get the picture. When you dance to the playlist, let your body intuitively respond in movement to the energy of each piece of music.

What I like about movement is that whatever move you make, you create a new neural pathway. It's like having a triple bonus. You're doing something good for your brain and physical fitness, expanding your self-expression, and having fun.

When I talk to groups, I ask people how they want to feel when they speak. Not how they want to be viewed, but how they want to feel. We make a list. It usually includes things such as feeling balanced, grounded, playful, passionate, strong, serene, focused, alive. Which ones speak to you? What would you add?

You can take your list of qualities, find a matching piece of music, and dance that quality into being. If you want to feel balanced, explore balance in your movement. If you want to feel impassioned, dance into that.

You can't call upon something if it's not available and accessible. Expand your repertoire with movement, befriend your body and how it expresses itself, and it will be on hand to back up your speaking in a natural and authentic way.

Facial Expressions

Many of us are conditioned to have poker faces. Don't show, don't tell. Hiding your feelings can be protective and, in some cases, offer you an advantage—for instance, when you are in negotiations. A relaxed countenance is also a sign of composure. I've consciously cultivated "Buddha nature" inside myself in order to respond to stress with calm and equanimity. Given my tense and fearful background, this new habit of serenity has helped me move through life able to breathe freely.

There are other upsides to a serene countenance. The absence of big, visible reactions can create a safe space for others. As a leader, coach, or consultant, maintaining composure keeps the focus on the other person and makes it less about you.

However, the downside is that people may not know what you are thinking. We naturally look at expressions to help us with the context of what a speaker is saying. So when you want to communicate clearly, if you don't use your face, you are leaving "money on the table" in communication currency.

Facial expressions help the listener create connections both with the material and with you as a person. When you allow yourself to respond internally to what you are speaking about, you can show warmth, enthusiasm, passion, disgust, amusement, and any other nuanced emotion. It also can add to the entertainment value.

You can play with this right now. As you read, allow your face and body to respond to the words, ideas, and meaning.

The girl's group Trio Mandili from the Republic of Georgia have created quite a splash on YouTube. They sing their traditional songs as they walk down dusty roads with rural scenes in the background. Most viewers don't understand the lyrics. But what captures us beyond the haunting tunes and voices are the cheeky personalities of the singers. The lead singer, in particular, makes all kinds of facial expressions as her two companions sing their solo lines. I presume she's responding to the meaning of the lyrics. In any case, it's charming.

If you are a contributor in a meeting or on a panel, your facial expressions can support and add to the person speaking even when you're not saying anything. Don't check out just because it's someone else's turn to speak. When you show interest, enthusiasm, surprise, or concurrence, your thoughtfulness comes through. What results is something more interesting for the audience, for sure. It also keeps you present and engaged. Plus, your responsive countenance offers you yet another opportunity to express yourself and enjoy the experience.

The Embodied Speaker

There is no one right way to move as a speaker. Some talks call for stillness, others for animation. You'll likely include both stillness and movement depending on the content you share, the stories you tell, the emotion you want to convey.

I suggest that you move when it helps you illustrate the story or when you want to connect with different sections of the audience. Many speakers move to discharge their nervous energy. That may work for you but can be distracting for the audience. An exception would be if pacing is a part of your story or intentionally a part of your brand. Comedian Trevor Noah paces as he builds up the tension in the story. But you know that it's completely planned out.

There's no right or wrong way to use your body. What you are aiming for is comfort inside your skin and to find ways to connect and communicate with your audience.

When your body feels familiar, when you trust and enjoy the movements that appear, you will be grounded and centered whether you are sitting in a chair, standing in front of a group, or onstage in a theater.

Un-fill the Filler Words

Many of my clients come to me distressed by their habit of using filler words. They see themselves on video or they go to Toastmasters and are told that they use too many of these words. It's true that when overused, they can be problematic. If you feel dismay every time you hear yourself utter "um," the self-criticism can make you feel self-conscious and discourage you as you speak. For the listener, a sentence punctuated with too many "ums" can make the meaning hard to follow.

Before we work on eliminating your filler words, however, let's again take a look under the hood at why they might be there in the first place. You never know, you might find another circumstance to declutter from your psychic closet.

Saying "um" has several useful features. If your teacher just called on you and you're caught off guard, saying "um" buys you time to collect your thoughts and come up with a creative response, if not the one the teacher is looking for. It's also useful as a space holder. It keeps others from butting in. The fear may be that if you pause in silence, it will signal to others you are finished and they're welcome to take the mic.

Because of my years in music, I have a pet theory that the vibration in the sound might also serve to stimulate the brain in some way. Whether this last bit is true or not, this habit served an important function.

What served you earlier on, though, may no longer be relevant. For instance, when you have the spotlight on you, when you are presenting or making a video, you have the mic all to yourself. You don't have to worry about being interrupted by others. You can, in fact, pause to think. But since "um" has become a habit, you'll need to repattern.

The practice of Embodied Connection will help you with your filler words, as will the exploration of speech sound-making. You will be present and fully in the moment of your speaking and on the lookout to land your sentences with strong words. You'll be more comfortable taking silences to connect with yourself and your audience, including when you are in transition to a new thought. Silence will replace "um" when you need to think.

Your practice and play with sounds and words as well as your emphasis on and expression of the words will also anchor you into the freshness of the moment so that your ideas spring forth more readily, or at least comfortably, while you're forming what you want to say. If you have practiced your script with delicious diction, your muscle memory will help roll the words off your tongue.

What I'm saying here is that as you develop connection to your somatic and vocal confidence, your overuse of filler words will be a thing of the past.

Use Video as a Tool

When one of my college dance professors moved out of the area, he bequeathed me his reel-to-reel video player. This was a huge gift, and a heavy one too, maybe twenty-five pounds. It was complicated to run as well, threading the tape around spools. But what a great tool it was! Several years later, when I was choreographing for my own dance ensemble, I recorded the troupe's movements with this piece of equipment, and watched it later at home to evaluate, and decide what worked and what needed to change or happen next. I felt lucky. Very few people had equipment like this to work with.

Today, everyone has such a gadget. Take out your phone and use it. Use it as a tool for learning, exploring, experimenting. Take any of the exercises in this chapter and do them on video. It will be endlessly entertaining, and you will grow by leaps and bounds in your self-expression.

The Spice Cabinet

You won't be bringing everything you explore into a speaking moment. You may not want or need to be goofy, for instance, in a presentation. However, you might enjoy being goofy telling a story at a party.

It's like cooking. You won't use every item you have in your cabinets for every dish. Some items might get used often, like salt, olive oil, and garlic. Other ingredients get pulled out for particular dishes or occasions. You may not use basil or cumin all the time, but having it stocked makes cooking easier and more flavorful.

By stretching out your range, you increase the number of ingredients available to you. Just like items in the kitchen, if you don't open the fridge and the cabinets, you may not remember what's inside and available to use.

Expression isn't something that is "one and done." As humans, we continually evolve in our self-expression. Just as your familiarity and ease on a guitar will build when you mess around on it a lot, so will your familiarity with your creative and free self-expression build as you experiment and stretch.

Keep in mind, too, the benefit for your audience. Remember the mirror neurons in us all? People watching and listening to you will resonate and light up in those same places in their brains as you do when you express yourself.

There is a reason for the expression, "smile and the whole world smiles with you." When you pass someone in the street with a grin across their face, happy as heck, it makes you smile too.

START WITH THIS

Make three lists.

In the first, write down the words your good friends and colleagues would use to describe what they see, like, and appreciate in you. If you don't know, ask. Tell them your coach gave you this assignment.

Then make a list of what other words you'd love to hear in addition. In other words, how would you love to grow in your expression?

For your third list, write down a few ways you could practice in your day to day life.

13

Prepare the Way for
the Words You Say

"It's not our job to be clever or smart, but to connect."
MICHAEL PORT

WHETHER YOU SPEAK extemporaneously or memorize a script, if you don't feel prepared or comfortable with the form, you will experience anxiety. If you are prepared with what to say, are well familiarized with your topic, or have practiced spontaneous speaking, you'll possess a sense of certainty, control, and predictability.

How we prepare for a speaking experience can greatly impact the outcome. Of course, preparation has to do with what you will be saying—your content. You also prepare mentally, physically, and emotionally. There are two times you'll spend preparing: way in advance and immediately before speaking, or close to the time you speak.

Not all speaking situations call for the same preparation, and not all styles of preparation are right for everyone.

Preparing for a conversation will be different from preparing for a TV interview and different from preparing a talk for the stage. How you prepare for a livestream on social media will be different from how you prepare for a professional video shoot. Some of the same preparation, though, can be used for any of these. In this chapter, I'll show you how to prepare mentally, physically, and emotionally for speaking in a way that makes it a joyful activity in and of itself.

Improvisation and "Winging It"

Most of the speaking we do in life is extemporaneous. From the time we hit the kitchen in the morning until we close our eyes at night, we "wing" our way through life. For the times you are in the limelight, though, when more than one person is on the listening end, there are things you can do to prepare for the best outcome.

We have all kinds of speaking experiences throughout our day. On one end of the spectrum is the completely unplanned, like the conversations you have with family, friends, and neighbors at the coffee shop. On the other end is a script. In between are all the gradations.

We tend to think of conversations as spontaneous, though some are not. Have you ever rehearsed a conversation in your head ahead of time? For years, before I ever had a child, I would run certain conversations through my head that I imagined I would have should I ever have a teen kid— conversations about sex and drugs and cautionary tales from mistakes made. Years later, I did have these conversations, and I was actually well prepared from all my years of periodic rehearsal in my head.

Many business conversations are also well planned. If you provide services or programs or products, you have sales conversations that are rehearsed, at the very least, from experience and repetition.

Sometimes, though, you are called upon to "take the stage" unexpectedly, and you feel put on the spot. At a party, your friend calls you over and says, "Tell Courtney about the time you had to jump off the cliff." Or the person on your team who was going to present to management had to bring their kid to the doctor and suddenly you have to fill in for them. Or the local TV station calls you as an expert on ways you can boost your immune system with superfoods during flu season. In these times, you may have little or no time to prepare. You compose yourself, get out there, and do the best you can to fulfil the needs of the occasion. You "wing it."

The expression "to wing" comes from the theater world. It describes the actor who is called in at the last minute and is either learning their lines in the wings—those side curtains onstage—before going out onstage or they are out onstage already and someone in the wings is feeding them their lines in a whisper.

Although the original meaning of the expression has a neutral meaning, in the speaking world, it carries a negative connotation among some. The objection is that the presenter didn't care enough about the audience to prepare.

I personally am not so quick to judge. Sometimes, the circumstances in our lives are such that we have no choice. Or maybe planning, organizing, getting into the nitty-gritty of preparation feels hard to do.

Some clients confess to me that they don't prepare because every time they go to work on their presentation, it brings up anxiety. It feels easier to just go out there, wing it, and hope for the best. At least then they are only suffering for that short period of time. Hopefully by now you no longer need to avoid preparation because of the fear.

Still other speakers say they like to wing it because they feel more natural when what they have to say is unplanned.

Michael Port, co-founder and CEO of Heroic Public Speaking, explains the problem of winging it in order to feel natural. He argues that when you wing it, there may be times when you feel like you are brilliant, but more often than not, you'll perform suboptimally. Winging it produces sporadic results. Preparation, however, produces consistency and consistent opportunities to be brilliant.

I totally agree. But there will undoubtedly be times when you'll have no choice but to wing it. You'll be on a panel discussion or taking questions, and something will come at you that is outside your well-trodden stories or ideas. Kit Pang of BostonSpeaks runs many panel events and enjoys the spontaneity that happens with unexpected questions. He purposefully poses surprise and random questions to the panel to liven things up.

If it's inevitable that you are going to have to wing it at some point, to some degree, let's look at how you can excel. Although "improvise" is often used interchangeably with "winging it," improvisation is a practiced art form. Dance improvisation, musical improvisation, improv theater, speaking improvisation—they are practiced.

I used to choreograph dance as well as create improvised performances. My interest was to create a choreography that captured the spontaneity of improvisation but also to make my improvisation feel choreographed. That is, I wanted to take the spark of the moment and shape it as it unfolded in such a way that it made sense and had a journey rather than seeming rambling and random.

Improvisation can be structured and based on predetermined rules. In musical improvisation, you might begin with a chord structure and then add a melody on top. Or you might have a "conversation" between two players, with one offering a melodic or rhythmic line and then getting a response from the other.

In creative movement, you might have a structure to explore physically moving toward and away from a place, object, or person. Or the rule might be, as in Authentic Movement, to simply close your eyes and see what movement wants to arise.

If you want to think better on your feet, if you want to be better at knowing what to say in different situations, practice your speaking improvisation. In my programs, we might begin with Embodied Connection, as described in chapter 10. Embodied Connection is when you take a moment to look inward for somatic and energetic connection to yourself, and then outward for this same connection but with your audience.

After anchoring themselves in their body, each person takes a turn speaking from a prompt, a question, or even speaking in a stream of consciousness, as you might do when writing in your journal. We follow it up with positive reflections—what we like and appreciate about the speaker's energy and essence, what was said, how it was said, and so on. In this way, each speaker gets to know what is strong and impactful, and builds trust in themselves.

You can do this in other ways. Take an improv class. Take opportunities you already have in your life to practice casual speaking—with friends and family at home, with colleagues at breaks or lunchtime, at conferences where you meet new people, on virtual chats and chance encounters on the street. Practice sharing your ideas and points of view.

If you practice with self-awareness, you'll clock hours of experience. Here's what I mean by self-awareness:

- Practice Embodied Connection. Get in the habit of connecting with yourself to feel grounded and relaxed. Feel into your connection with others. Speak from that place of connection. When you think too hard, you inadvertently create tension. When you aren't speaking, clear your mind. Listen and widen your awareness to take in more of your external environment as well as track your inner state of being.

- Notice what you like to share about, the details you go into, and what you omit and leave out.

- Challenge yourself to be concise. Stop before you give a complete dissertation on the topic; leave others with a sense of curiosity and space to ask questions.

- Ask questions of your own to bring out responses to your ideas: "What's your take on this topic? Have you ever had this experience?"

- When you share an idea or the same story on different occasions, change it up by stretching the story out with more detail, or shrinking it down to the bare bones.

- Listen to yourself as you speak and let yourself enjoy the experience of speaking. Allow yourself to play with your expression, sound-making, and delivery from the last chapter. At the very least, think about amplifying what you are already doing just a bit, like 5 or 10 percent. The more you practice speaking with nonjudgmental observation and awareness, the better you'll get at speaking on the spot.

- Keep your ears open for a great sentence to end on that has power and stick it like a gymnast on her dismount. In other words, when you hear a good place to stop, simply close your mouth and offer silence.

In this way, when you are called upon to improvise or wing it, you'll actually be practiced enough to speak with the naturalness you had in your conversations. Because you'll be familiar with what works, what you like to do, how people are likely to respond and be impacted by what you say, you'll already be aware of speaking in a concise manner and ending strong.

Networking and Attending Workshops

Networking. Some people love it. Many people hate it and find it stressful. But it can be fun and a practice space for your speaking. When you network, you have a perfect opportunity to do some market research—you can test ideas and see what people's responses are. Networking events and workshops offer you two elements of speaking experiences: one-on-one conversations and standing in the spotlight for a short amount of time. We'll look at each of these in turn.

The Conversation

The bulk of networking is in the form of one-on-one conversations during which you turn to someone and ask about their work, and they, in turn, will ask about what you do. There are more conversation starters than this, but at some point, this is where it leads to—what you do.

You might fret about this and think, *I never know what to say!* Well then, this is where preparation helps. Think about it ahead of time. In your journal, write, "When someone asks me about what I do, I'm going to say X." Have the attitude of research here, that you are going to try something and evaluate the data that you collect—data about how it felt to say what you did, how it was responded to, what you might try the next time.

When I first went to networking events with no experience and little awareness, I thought that when it was my turn to speak, I had to explain everything I did all at once. As soon as someone asked me what I did, I dove into a very long, detailed explanation. More than once, the person who asked me the question nodded politely while I droned on and on, and then excused themselves to get food or visit the restroom. What was the data I collected? Too many words.

I've learned that saying less is more effective. A few years back, I met up with an online friend who lived in Malta, where I was vacationing for a few days. We found an outdoor restaurant with a view of the Mediterranean.

While we waited for our salad, I turned to her British boyfriend and asked, "So what do you do?"

"I'm in gambling." He said the words and then closed his mouth. Do you think I wanted to know more? Hell, yeah!

I now like to see how I can explain what I do in one sentence. If the listener is interested, they ask questions or tell me a story of their own experience. It's actually more valuable to hear what your conversation partner has to say about your topic. It shows that they relate to it.

I recommend you experiment with intention. See what happens when your description of what you do is super-short, and see what happens when you say two or three sentences. Try telling them the industry, and another time, more specifically, who you help or what you do in your company. Gather your data and continue to try things out. Of course, this is not going to be a perfect experiment. Everyone you speak to will be in a different relationship to your topic. Cultivate an attitude of nonattachment and curiosity.

At the beginning of my networking experience, I also made the mistake of being too self-referential. This is when someone shares their experience and you immediately come back with how that reminds you of something in your own experience. Some of that is okay. It's one of the ways we connect. It may also be useful to the person you are speaking with *if* you are their ideal customer or client. But when you do that all the time, when you always respond with how something relates to your life, it makes the person you're talking to feel as if you are more interested in yourself than in them. Rather than turn the conversation to yourself, ask follow-up questions. Invite your speaking partner to go a little deeper.

And if you find yourself always the one asking questions and your partners are only too happy to talk about themselves and never ask you about you, this is your moment to nod politely and excuse yourself to get a drink.

The Network Spotlight

Depending on the size of the event, the host will call everyone to gather in a circle to share about you or your work in a "go-around" format. I used to have a strange feeling come over me as it got closer to my turn to speak. Maybe it's happened to you too. It was as if my body separated and floated a few feet above myself and I was not quite sure what I was saying.

Because you are generally in a room of peers, this is most likely a trigger from being in school or possibly a large family where you felt unsafe or unseen. Think about the classroom, when the teacher would go around to each student and you were put on the spot to come up with the right answer; maybe you were often unprepared and worried about being good enough and whether you'd be seen as smart or stupid. If you feel anxious in this kind of situation and you didn't address this as you read chapter 4, now's your time to go back to resolve and clear this influencing experience.

Network Confidence

Before you head out to a networking event or workshop, spend a few moments to prepare yourself. Decide how you want to answer the inevitable question, "So, what do you do?" It's going to happen. Think about how you have answered that question in the past. Try out something a little different. Let yourself use this opportunity to experiment.

The same goes for when you attend a workshop. Often, if it is a small enough group, the presenter will ask people to introduce themselves and say something about how the topic is relevant to them. To prepare yourself, write down the following prompts.

- The reason I'm going to this workshop is _____
  _____

- What I want to learn about is _____
  _____ .

- This is relevant to me at this time because_____

_____

When you have what you want to say already in mind, when others are speaking you can simply listen, get to know who is in the room, and trust that when it's your turn to speak, you will be prepared with what you want to say.

Preparing Your Script

Too many talks are not well prepared for. I can understand why this happens. You may not know how to go about it. Preparation seems like a hard thing and not fun at all. I used to feel that way too. I used to not know what I wanted to say or how to say it effectively.

Now, I feel differently. Partially because I've devoted a lot of time to scriptwriting. And I've gotten help.

Michael and Amy Port say that when you write a script that changes your own life as well as that of others, you have to dig deep to find the truth of your idea and you have to expect it to be challenging.

Given this challenge, you might wonder if you should work with somebody on your script. If you can afford it, yes! As someone who always struggled with finding "the words to say it," I found working with writing and speaking coaches to be invaluable. I would encourage you to find a speaking program that will help you not only with script creation but also with coaching on the stage to broaden your skills, particularly if you have a dream of speaking at conferences regularly as part of your work.

If investing in this type of support isn't an option for you, read books (I list my favorites in the bibliography at the end of this book) and study the speakers you listen to, at events and online. Become attentive to what you like and find effective.

Writing out your words will ground you and organize your thoughts. A script or outline will take the stress off your brain about what to say. Speaking program or not, know that bringing a talk to life that you love takes time, experience, and iteration. Try it out in front of lots of different audiences. Speaker Andrew Davis says that when he develops a new talk, he tries to give it twelve times within a month! Twelve times gives you enough repetition to know your script well and to refine it bit by bit. Remember to hold yourself in your process with unconditional friendliness, and as much as you can, think of the process as play to make it fun and interesting.

Speaking with Notes

If you're giving a one-time speech, you may want to rely on notes. Don't mistake using notes for simply reading aloud. Reading from notes doesn't exempt you from preparation. The only exception is if you were given something to read at the last moment that you've never seen before. Even then, you can utilize the expressiveness in your delivery to help the listener make meaning of what you are reading. This requires you to slow down enough to make meaning of it for yourself.

I remember many occasions when I had to read aloud in school. I know I said the words correctly, but I had no idea of what I was saying. Zero comprehension. Zero! Somehow the teacher couldn't tell or didn't care about the disconnect between my brain and my mouth. I certainly didn't feel safe enough to tell her. It was only when I became a mom and read endlessly to my daughter and wanted *her* to enjoy and understand what I was saying that I also began to understand the words I read out loud.

Whether you create a script to read from or to eventually memorize, there are practices that can bring enjoyment to the preparation experience and lead to a satisfying performance.

I go through my entire script with a single intention each time. Each intentional step is fun to do and familiarizes me with the language on a deeper level as I explore how I can deliver the lines. And each time I run through a script, I learn it a little bit more. In this way, if I am going to be reading, I won't be glued to my paper but instead can look up into the lens or the eyes of someone in the audience. And if I am aiming to memorize, following this list gives me the repetition I need without the boredom. Here's the plan:

1   The first intentional step is the obvious one: read through your script out loud and note where you question the phrasing. It might look good on paper, but if it doesn't sound like how you would speak it, you'll need to make changes.

2   Get to know what every word feels like in your jaw and on your tongue and lips, as we did in chapter 11. Speak the words slowly, feeling all the vowels and consonants resonate in your mouth until they feel fluid. Make sure the words roll off your tongue easily. If you get stuck on a phrase, say it slowly to enunciate the consonants and vowels. This will groove the vocal actions into your physical memory, so you don't stumble over words.

3 Read each sentence numerous times to explore the different words and phrases you can emphasize, as you did in the "I Don't Care Game" from chapter 11. We tend to have habitual inflections. Playing around with discovering how each sentence could be said helps you create more variation.

4 Go back through your script to find what feels natural to your speaking tone. Imagine there is a friend sitting across a table from you and you are speaking these words to them. Better yet, get together with a friend and deliver it to them over dinner.

5 You know how you read a children's book with different voices for the different characters? Do that with your script. Read it through in different characters and accents.

6 Read it as fast as you can. Try to maintain your expressiveness. I learned this from Amy Port, co-founder and president of Heroic Public Speaking, and have found it forces me to coordinate my mouth muscles and vocal cords. It also highlights the places that are harder for me to say, so I can go over them again.

7 Sing your words, like you're a singer-songwriter, singing an opera, rock, or rap.

8 Move your body, dancing as you speak through your script, letting the movement inspire and amplify how you deliver the words.

Going through your script with this intentional awareness can be a delicious and hilarious process of exploring the words and your ways of expressing them. That you won't ever use most of what you come up with is beside the point. The point is that the words become embodied and experienced deeply in a holistic way.

To Memorize or Not to Memorize, That Is the Question

There are times to memorize a talk word for word, and there are times it's not necessary or advised. If you have a TED talk, are in a storytelling competition, at a pitch fest, or are giving a five-minute Insight talk, where there is a strict time limit and you will be disqualified if you go over, memorizing a talk word for word is a good idea. If you have a signature talk that you give over and over, you may want to memorize it (or you'll find that you've memorized it by virtue of repetition).

Memorizing is a commitment. To do it well takes a long runway of time. If you are going to memorize, begin far in advance. Even a ninety-second memorized video ad is going to take time to learn by heart—several days to a week would be helpful. It's hard to relax and freely express yourself when your brain is working overtime to remember the next lines.

That's why some people keep a stack of note cards with them, just in case. If it helps you feel more relaxed, do this too. You can have the big outline, the talking points, key ideas, or stories, one on each card, and use them to remind you what comes next.

Some speakers resist memorization, fearing that it will sound stiff. If a script is only partially memorized so that you are working to remember, then yes, it may sound stiff.

Seth Godin says, "It's not because people memorize too much, it's because they don't memorize enough. Watch a great performance and you'll see no artifacts of memoriza-tion. Instead, you will see someone speaking from the heart. This is what it means to *know something by heart.* Memoriz-ing the words is half of it."

When you know a script inside and out, you can play with it. Think of a song you can sing from start to finish. You can sing your heart out, right? That's how you want to feel with a memorized script.

In my music group, we never perform with the written music. Occasionally, someone will have a word card. But director Susan Robbins always said that the real rehearsal starts after a piece is memorized. You want to be fully in the music and able to express it. It needs to be yours, in your heart.

The same is true with a script. Take on the attitude that you are just beginning the real work of a piece when it's already memorized. When you learn something by heart, so that it's in you, really in you, not halfway memorized, there is a freedom. You can play with it.

The other complaint about memorization is that the words don't feel as natural as extemporaneous speech. This may be because the script you wrote isn't based on your natural speaking. We are taught to write in an academic or literary way that doesn't reflect speech patterns. When you write a script, you'll need to say it out loud with an ear to how you would say it in conversation. That's why I encour-age you to consciously speak about your ideas in casual settings, so that you can explore and discover the ways you naturally communicate your ideas.

It's hard to fully appreciate how long it takes to memorize something well. Most people miscalculate. I have too, espe-cially since I count on deadlines to motivate me to bump a task up on my priority list. Through the experience of not giving myself enough time to memorize, I've better learned how much time I need.

If you are going to memorize, give yourself more time than you think you need and make your deadline well in advance of your talk, even by a week or two. Practicing words up until the time you are to speak will mean that most of your attention will be on word recall as opposed to communication, connection, and presence.

I know life happens. You may find yourself absorbed in the words until the last minute anyway. At some point, though, you have to let go of what you had hoped for and find the most optimum with what you have.

Tips for Memorization

The two most popular memorization hacks are the memory palace and mnemonics. The memory palace is where you associate words or ideas with places in a space, like different rooms in your home, or in a town where you always pass the storefronts in the same order. Mnemonics use pictures, patterns of letters, or associations to cue your memory.

These hacks take time in themselves to learn so, perhaps because of my impatience, I prefer to work directly with a script. Script memorization can be a creative activity. Plus, as I mentioned above, the more you play with your script, the more familiar it becomes and the more fun it is to deliver.

Start off by following the steps earlier in the chapter for reading your notes. If you run through those passes first, you may already have a ninety-second video script memorized. If you have a twenty-minute talk or longer, then follow these next steps.

1   Record yourself speaking the script on your phone. Then play it in the car when you drive, or listen to it while you do chores, when you're out for a walk, or when you lie in bed. Just listen to the overall piece to become familiar with it, as if you are listening to someone else's talk. This is a good opportunity to discover places in your script you want to refine. If you find yourself tuning out, record the sections in different character voices.

2   Before you try to memorize an entire talk, chunk down your script into five to seven natural sections. Name them and memorize the order. Once you have the big picture memorized, create sections within each chunk and memorize those. Sometimes I'll color code my pages for visual support.

3   Once you know this outline, you can work line by line. Everyone tends to start at the beginning. That's natural, and you also want to start strong, so go ahead and start with the beginning. Listen to the section and then try your hand at recall. You can try to speak along with the recording. Or you can play one line at a time and speak it back. Or just work with your written script. Say one sentence and look back to see that you've got it as written. Say it again and again. Then add another sentence.

4   Skip to the end. Most people work through a script in order, which means the end of the talk gets short shrift. But the end of the talk is the last impression people will have. Make it a strong lasting impression.

5   Turn on your camera and practice your sections one at a time. Watch back to determine your next improvements.

6 Practice your lines while washing dishes, gardening, or taking a walk. Practice speaking to your pet.

If you create a talk that you will give only once, does it make sense to go through all of this trouble? It depends on the stakes, the expected protocol, the time you have, and the wow factor you are aiming to achieve. For instance, most TED stages want their talks to be memorized regardless of length.

Even if you have a talk that you will give over and over, it's natural that it will evolve over time. You might wonder, then, if it makes sense to memorize something that's in flux. Good point! In that case, Michael and Amy Port make the suggestion to memorize ideas rather than just words. I've used this hybrid approach: I memorize the first and last sections and my key stories. Then each time I give the talk, sometimes twice or three times in a week, I commit to memorizing another small piece, until I have the entire talk memorized.

Memorization will also come in handy for short, important videos, when you want the exact words and also to optimize your connection to the viewer. You can use a teleprompter app, of course, but these present a few problems. First, most of us have a reading voice and a speaking voice. It takes practice and awareness to get the words you read to sound like the words you speak. Second, while your eyes are focused on reading, they are not focused on the lens and the person watching. This can be practiced as well. Look at the words with the same open-hearted connection that you would when you look at someone you care about. See the words as people.

When you play with your script in these ways, not only do you have it in your mind, but it also becomes part of your neurophysiology, so it rolls off your tongue. You can feel relaxed and be present with your audience, play with your delivery, and give a heartfelt performance with presence.

START WITH THIS

Suggest a topic to talk about with your family, a group of friends, colleagues, or students. You can say, "I've been thinking about gratitude lately [or kindness, or equality or whatever!], and I'm curious how you see it in your life or how it applies to your business. Let's go around and have a turn to share our thoughts." You can use a timer or not. After each person shares, you can say what you liked and appreciated in it or not. You can go off on tangents, but be sure that everyone present has their turn in the limelight.

14

Delight in the Limelight

"When you invite the universe to support you,
you get connected to the source of all things,
and you can gracefully move beyond your limitations."
OPRAH WINFREY

OME DECADES AGO, I read about the all-night dance rituals of the !Kung people ("!" indicates a tongue click) of the Kalahari. In his book *Boiling Energy*, anthropologist Richard Katz describes how three times a week, these small tribes stayed up all night long around a fire, the women singing and clapping and the (mostly) men dancing in a circle for hours and hours in the hopes that one or several would fall into a trance. Once in the altered state of consciousness, this person gained special powers—the ability to see disease in people and draw it out. They also could see and argue with spirits on behalf of the tribe. The journey into the trance was arduous, but the dancers persisted for the health and well-being of their tribe, and the community was present to support the dancers' journey in all ways.

Although this otherworldly account is far outside my experience, there are aspects that I can liken to the Zar ritual dance I performed with my women's world music group. This pre-Islamic healing practice is still used today across North Africa and in parts of the Middle East for when one feels "dis-ease" in some way. When I performed it in New Delhi, India, several audience members assured me that a dance like this could be found there too.

During the Zar, with closed eyes, you allow the spirit that is associated with various drum rhythms to "move" you. It's a dialogue between you and the spirit, which has been out of alignment. As you give yourself over to the music, you and the spirit become reconnected.

The bass drum begins. *Dum, ta doom tek, Dum ta dum tek!* I let my head drop and lift to the lilt of the rhythm. It's a subtle movement. A simple drop and lift to one side, then the other. I let the beat hook into me. I follow its guidance. One by one, other instruments add their tones to the deep boom of the bass drum, and as the beat moves on, the percussionists split into new rhythms that beckon my shoulders to move, and then an arm.

I hold myself back. No hurry. We are in another time, another place. I patiently await the tinkles of the finger cymbals to awaken my hands and fingertips. Although my feet are firmly planted on the wooden stage, my upper body sways as it's carried by the tempo that inexorably moves forward, faster, earnest, desiring, pleading, faster and faster until the movement threatens chaos and I drop to my knees in a frenzied finish of release on the floor.

Everything goes silent. My heart pounds against my knees as I grant myself a few breaths to settle in the silence— but not too long or the audience will start to worry.

I've done this dance many, many times over three decades, maybe three hundred times. Although as a group we felt ready to swap out that piece of the repertoire, our director kept it in. "The state of the world needs it," she said. It always seemed the state of the world needed this kind of experience.

After each performance, people seek me out, look into my eyes, and tell me that no matter how many times they see this dance, it brings them to tears, though they don't know why. I don't know why either, except it breaks me open and I bring them with me. I do it for them. It's my offering.

Something happens because others are there to witness. I go to the place I go to not just by letting them see me but *because* they see. Because their eyes, attention, hope, desire, and buried grief await the descent so that together we can all open up in the way we each need.

Imagine speaking being like this. That the presence of the audience and their attention on you provides the focus and energy for you to shift into a state where you benefit the people there as well as yourself.

At the beginning of this book, perhaps your first and only desire was to overcome your fear of speaking. If you've read through this book and tried the exercises, maybe you feel you've achieved some movement in that direction. And when you began the book, perhaps you couldn't imagine this kind of deep exchange with your audience, where both you and the audience were changed by the experience.

Even everyday meetings and conversations can be satisfying, meaningful, and fun. On the spiritual end, it can be an ecstatic peak experience, one that is repeatable or at least has high odds of happening because you create the environment for it to happen.

You've been learning all along in this book how to create that environment. You've learned how to clear away the elements from your past that triggered your fear response, so you could catch up to yourself in this present time. You've learned to create a safe environment inside and around you so that you feel an unconditional friendliness toward yourself that encourages and forgives. You've expanded your capacity to connect both with yourself and your audience and embodied your self-expression down to the sounds of the words you speak. You've prepared your content and the practice of your delivery. You have led yourself through a guided visualization for speaking confidence.

Now, let's look at what you can do on the day of to remind yourself of all of these elements and maximize your experience.

Depending on the circumstance, you may not feel it's necessary to go through all of the steps here. If you have a high-stakes presentation, I suggest you carefully look at each of these pre-speaking rituals. Some are physical, some energetic, some use the imagination. You won't need to do them all each and every time—or you may want to! Let your intuition be your guide as you create your own readiness ritual. Any practice that attunes you to yourself, your body, your intentions, and your emotions, will serve you well. If you make it a habit to start your day with some of these practices, you will be tuned up and ready for all your spotlight moments from morning till night.

Physically Open Your Body and Face

The first place to begin your readiness is with your instrument—your physical body. You know now that you don't present with just your voice, that speaking is a whole-body experience. It's not enough that you stretched last week. Do it anytime you engage in speaking in an important way. If you spend a bit of time opening your body, you'll feel more physically ready, more grounded and confident, more energized, connected, and expressive.

You can simply stretch out your arms and legs, circle or twist your hips and back. You can run in place or put on some music and dance. Use these body connectors to awaken your body and promote a state of physical energized alertness. Pay attention, too, to your feet and legs. They are your connection to the earth.

Stretch your face as well, and your tongue. If no one is around to be frightened, you can do it right now as you read this! Open your mouth and eyes wide. Flick your tongue like a snake. When you make funny faces, you enliven the facial muscles. This will invite more expression as you speak with more dimension and energy in your communication.

You may think that if you speak on a podcast or webinar, where your face won't be seen, you can skip this step. Don't. When you open your body to be expressive, you'll feel the difference in your whole physical energy system, and your audience will feel it too.

Vocal Warm-Up

The voice again? Yes, the voice again! Just because you've played around with your voice to discover your range of expression, just because you've gone over your words with acute awareness of your articulation, doesn't mean you can gloss over the care of your voice on the day you present. At times, you can get away with not warming up your voice. Again, it totally depends on the situation. If a casual meeting is on the agenda and you feel confident, you may not feel it's necessary.

However, if you are presenting where you would previously feel nervous, definitely take time to connect with your vocal presence. After all, would you suggest that a musician skip the warm-up on their instrument before a concert? Probably not. As a speaker, your voice is your instrument.

Have you ever noticed that your voice is deeper in the morning when you wake up? Or raspy? Maybe you're a person not fit to talk until you've had your morning cup of tea or coffee. Singers notice that their voice is more open as the day goes on. If you want your voice to work well for you, it's important to allow a bit of time to make sure that the whole range you want to use is available to you. Let the stakes of the circumstance and the time of day dictate the time you spend preparing.

I recommend that you take five to fifteen minutes to fully explore what you can do with your voice. Go over the explorations you learned in chapter 11, "The Breath You Take and Sounds You Make." If you are traveling by car to a gig, you can warm up in the car. If you are in a hotel, you can warm up in your room.

Here's a quick review: Begin by finding a relaxed resonance on "Ah." Allow your tongue and jaw to be as relaxed as possible as you explore making a round and resonant sound. Then, as you maintain this relaxed resonance you just found, sing the words of your first speaking line on that same one pitch to feel a smoothness. Only speak as long as you have breath. Don't push the last words out. Instead, simply take your next breath and continue. If your sentence is too long for one breath, look for a comma, some natural break in the sentence, or create two shorter sentences from the one.

From there, say or sing your sentences by going lower and higher in pitch. Then play around with different tonalities: deep, twangy, light and airy, karate chop shout. When you come back to "just speaking," your voice will naturally have more expression because you took the time to "open the doors." And now your voice will be ready to go!

In the Zone

Now that you've taken care to prepare your body and vocal cords in a physical way, it's time to tune your state of being. You can create the conditions to get in the zone, where you feel powerful and focused, where your vibration is relaxed and open.

We subconsciously seek to adjust our energy all the time. For example, you feel tired, so you make a cup of coffee or decide to go for a walk. You may be in a crappy mood, but then you get a phone call from someone you're excited to hear from and your whole being lights up. You're in a rush to go somewhere, and as you step outside the door, sunshine blinds your eyes and you pause to savor the delicious warmth on your face.

If you want a particular kind of experience when you speak, cultivate it. Don't leave this to happenstance. Be intentional. The following practices can be thought of like an energetic stent: they open your energy so that you become the vehicle for your highest self, or something greater than you, to move through you unencumbered.

Intentional Energy

Think about the energy you want to bring to your presentation. Is it a sense of ease? Is it confidence or authority? Is it clarity, focus, spontaneity, eloquence, energy, openheartedness? Maybe playfulness or service? Invoke the energy you are looking to embody when you do your mental rehearsal.

Alternatively, create a playlist of music that invites and supports these qualities you want to embody. In your movement, explore what confidence feels like. You might feel it as powerful and strong, or as laid-back ease, jiving with the beat. Or both!

This ability to shift is within your power through your awareness, your movement, and your imagination. It doesn't matter so much which state of being you put yourself into. What's important is that it brings you into a state of expansion and feels good.

Next-Level Embodied Connection

With Embodied Connection, you learned to connect with yourself in the moment. You also made a connection with your audience, opened to receive their positive regard, and then expressed appreciation. Revisit this now again in your imagination. Invite every cell in your body to take part. Hold the space open for all the cells to be energized and nourished. What you are looking for is an energetic shift in your body, a natural high, an emotional/spiritual space that is alert and expansive yet relaxed, at ease, and, of course, connected.

When you make your body transparent to the energy of attention and let it come through you, there is a pleasure and enjoyment associated with it. You become attuned to a larger field of awareness that envelops the space and makes it sacred, a space where transfer and transformation can occur.

Chakra Meditation

I particularly enjoy the structure of chakra meditation to ready myself on all levels of being and to open to a larger field of awareness that goes beyond myself. The seven energy centers begin at the base of your spine or pelvis and move up through your body to the top of your head. Think of them in the center or core of your body. As you put your attention on each of these areas, invite these intentions to be activated:

* Base of your spine/pelvis: I am safe, secure, grounded, centered.

* Belly area: I honor my desire to speak, to serve, to expand into my full creative potential, to make an impact.

* Solar plexus: I call upon my strength and confidence, my persistence and inner authority.

* Heart: I open my heart to love and accept myself, and to connect with and serve my audience with understanding, empathy, and compassion.

* Throat: I open the door to my self-expression. May I be fully myself, and may the words that emerge be what my audience needs to hear.

* Third eye: My mind is clear, relaxed, and focused, open to both my intuitional and cognitive awareness.

* Top of head: I am open to being guided by the higher forces of the universe and trust that what I share is what needs to be heard today.

You can use this chakra meditation as you lie in bed, when you wake up the morning of your presentation. You can bring it into the shower with you. If you have some personal time before you present, you can do it then too.

Help from the Universe

Let's take a deeper look into the last chakra description of guidance from the "higher forces of the universe," whereby you become a vehicle for something to move through you. Maybe you've done absolutely everything you could think of to prepare for speaking, including all the suggestions I've offered in this book. Or maybe you didn't do as much as you would have liked.

In either case, when you get to the end of the time you have to prepare, I recommend you "hand it over." Hand it over to something greater than your everyday self. You could call it your higher self, or the greater forces of the universe. Call it God or Saraswati (look her up). Say, "I did what I could, and I'd love for you to support me the rest of the way and help me deliver the goods." After this surrender, you can see yourself as the vehicle to speak in such a way that the audience members get what they need from the experience. Some people describe this as a "download" in service to others, so that the people listening benefit by what you have to say. When you invite the universe to support you, it allows you to relax and be present, and, paradoxically, be at your best. Here are some suggestions for doing that:

* Forgive yourself for what you didn't do or forgot to do. Let it go. Honor the place you are in your journey. There is always next time.

- Trust that you are right where you are supposed to be in your journey. You may as well, because you can't be anywhere else than where you are.

- Let go of your attachment to the outcome. I'm not saying don't have goals or intentions that this speaking opportunity will have a certain result. I'm saying not to be attached to it. Just don't feel you "must" have this outcome or else, because maybe the universe has a different idea, or maybe there are things outside your control. And when you want this presentation to serve in a particular way, and you really, really want it—well, you can see already when I say you "really, really want it"—there's a physical tension, a mental and emotional tension. This tension will block your ability to be fully present and open to all your faculties.

  Rather, say, "I'd love this or something better for my greatest good and highest joy." When you let go in this way, you can feel at ease and you can be happy. And that's what I want for you. To feel happy in the limelight.

Touchstone Mantras

Sometimes you don't have time or the right environment in which to do an elaborate ritual. Or maybe you speak frequently, and you no longer have the need for an elaborate ritual but still want to honor the moment with intention. You can shorten any of these practices into what I call a "touchstone mantra." For instance, focus your attention on each of the chakras, one at a time, with a single word that encapsulates the energy you want to invoke. I might say, "Safety, desire, determination, heart, expression, awareness, trust." Use these or other words that have significance for you.

Brand and marketing consultant Gary Hirsch uses the phrase, "May I be helpful." When he says those words before he gives a pitch or leads a corporate workshop, it puts him into the frame of mind he's seeking.

Whatever ritual you use, seek to put yourself in the state of mind and body that will allow you to hit the ground running.

Quick Brain Reset

Brain Gym PACE exercises were developed for kids to increase learning readiness. PACE stands for positive, active, clear, and energetic. I find the exercises improve my concentration and focus. One is called Cross Crawl.

Basically, you march slowly in place for a minute, lifting one knee and then the other as you reach across your body to touch your knee with the opposite hand. Lift your left knee and reach across to touch it with your right hand. Then raise your right knee and reach across to touch it with your left hand. Your upper body will twist as you reach across.

Transformational kinesiologist Eliza Bergeson taught my music group, Libana, to use this exercise to put us into a state of readiness while we stood in the wings before a show or were waiting in the recording studio. Whenever someone felt their energy lagging, they would start the Cross Crawl, which would spread throughout the group.

You too can use this before you go on to speak, whether you have privacy or don't mind drawing attention.

For a stealth quick brain reset, use Brain Buttons. What I love about this exercise, other than that it works, is that you can do this in public surreptitiously. This simple movement will keep your attention and brain focused so you stay present and at the ready to speak. Spread apart your thumb and forefinger of one hand and place each under each side of your collarbone. Massage lightly. Place your other hand on your belly. Easy peasy. Whenever I do this exercise, I yawn. Don't be surprised if you yawn too.

Access videos of these PACE exercises plus one more on my readers' page on my website: delightinthelimelight.com/resources.

Presentation Presence in Person

Okay, so you've grounded and energized your body. You've sounded your vocal cords so your voice is ready to resonate. You've gotten mentally clear and focused. You've put yourself into a higher state of being. It's go time. You may think this moment should be some big thing, and yes, it is a big thing. I want to assure you, though, that you've taken care of it all. All of what you learned and explored in previous chapters was to expand your experience in this moment of presentation.

Here are simple reminders about your focus and awareness:

- You don't know what you'll find when you walk into a room for the first time. Become familiar with the space as you enter it. Look around at the walls, the windows, the corners and ceiling. Look at the seating arrangement and imagine people seated in various places. If people are already in the room, begin to connect with them. Either literally engage in conversation or with your senses to recognize their essence, send appreciation, and receive their positive regard in your imagination.

- Of course, your ability to connect specifically with folks will vary with the setting. A small meeting room invites connection differently from a theater, or online meeting platform.

- My friend Terri Trespicio sometimes walks onstage already speaking. That's her style. But if you want to ensure you feel grounded when you take the stage, give yourself a moment to center in the silence. Feel your body and the ground beneath your feet. Look at the audience— at one person, a few, or many, to acknowledge them. When you are connected to yourself, people will wait and even appreciate a moment or two of silent anticipation.

- On camera, the same Embodied Connection applies. If you can see the faces of the audience, take time to create your energetic connection to them. If you don't have visual access, feel the connection in your imagination. Remember that the lens is the doorway from your eyes to theirs. Look there.

- Begin to speak from this place of connection. Feel the physical sound and sensation of your words as they emerge and vibrate. Be one with your expression. What is fun, intriguing, exciting about your material? Show that in the way you deliver each word, sentence, and idea. When you are inside the telling, you will bring it to life.

- Your body is your friend in staying physically grounded. Use your mindful self-awareness to regulate the tension in your body. Notice the strength in your legs and how your feet meet the ground. As you connect with the ground and monitor tension, you'll regenerate your levels of relaxation and ease. Allow yourself to move, as it helps you tell your story or impart your talking or teaching points.

- Remember to let go and forgive yourself fast for any unintended lapses or skips in your content. No one but you will ever know what it was supposed to be unless you tell them. You can always weave back in material you skipped over or you can leave it out entirely. Or trust that what came out was the way it was meant to be. Maybe it's even better than the original!

- Remember, too, to refuel. Take moments of silence to let you and your audience catch up on what's been said. And to feel a moment together. If you cover lots of data and concepts, a pause provides space to integrate.

- If there is applause, you know what to do—take it in. Have a blast!

Peak Experience

This experience can feel good. Very good. Like a special honor. When you trust yourself and what will emerge, when you have cleared the emotional blocks, when you tune up your energy to expand out instead of contract in, when you enjoy the sound and sensation of your voice blended with the words and meanings with people there to listen, the experience can be exhilarating: a natural high not just in the presence of others but *because* of the presence of others. You can do more and reach higher because of the limelight. You do it for yourself as you let yourself be seen. You do it for others, to serve.

START WITH THIS

Create your own pre-speaking ritual by going back through this chapter and choosing two to four practices that resonate with you. Write them on a card that you keep handy for your spotlight moments.

CONCLUSION

"There is a vitality, a life force, a quickening that is translated through you into action, and because there is only one of you in all time, this expression is unique. And if you block it, it will never exist through any other medium and be lost. The world will not have it."

MARTHA GRAHAM

IN THE MID-NINETIES, I became obsessed with a new passion: raw milk. My sister turned me on to it. She had adopted a child and made her own baby formula with a base of raw milk. I was intrigued, so I researched. I learned that raw milk contains beneficial bacteria, which explains why the milk my husband drank in his native Hungary could clabber when left at room temperature. He said this yogurt-like product was relished by the elderly and good for when you were sick. When he tried to clabber the pasteurized milk here in the States, it would just turn rotten. Mystery solved! Plus, according to some studies, raw milk protects against asthma and allergies.

More than the science, though, I got to thinking how, as a nursing mom, I would never consider processing my breast milk before feeding my child. Studies show that pasteurizing breast milk significantly reduces its protective antimicrobial properties. Moreover, unprocessed milk has been consumed for centuries, and owning a cow or a herd was considered a sign of wealth. Today across Europe, there are even raw-milk vending machines, over a thousand in Italy alone! Let's just say I was hooked.

I started making phone calls to farmers across the state to ask if I could purchase a gallon. Every single one politely informed me they weren't allowed to sell raw milk in Massachusetts—it was illegal. So, I called the state health commissioner to find out why. Let me tell you: he was furious that I'd even *dare* to ask about such a dangerous substance. I held the phone away from my head to protect my eardrums.

But I was obsessed. I had to get raw milk. The search continued. And that's how I ended up talking to Julie Rawson, the director of the Northeast Organic Farming Association.

"Julie," I said, "there's got to be a way for people like me to buy raw milk from licensed dairies. I believe this is a cause that the organic farming community should take on."

Without a hint of resistance, she said, "You're right, Linda. I'll give you two minutes to give a short address before the keynote speaker at our summer conference. There will be twelve hundred people there." I felt the blood drain from my brain. My mind immediately shot back to grad school: the dry mouth, the pitiful looks on the faces of the department heads.

"Please," I said, "can you do it instead of me? I can't speak in front of a crowd." But she wouldn't have it.

"You're the one with the knowledge and passion," she said. "Just write it out on a page and read it. You'll be fine."

I did what Julie told me to do. I spent the two weeks leading up to the conference, heart palpitating, writing and rewriting that one page. I read it out loud firmly in front of the mirror. On that balmy evening in August, I stood next to the stage, shaking like a leaf, waiting to be called up to the podium. Faced with those twelve hundred people, I was terrified. What would they think? Was I crazy? Would they boo me? Throw tomatoes? I walked up the wobbly aluminum steps to the stage, lay down my paper on the podium, and started to read. I remembered to look out at the audience, but truthfully, I saw nothing. I got to the end of my talk and then it happened... wild applause! I thought, *Yes! I did this.* I felt proud and joyful and overwhelmingly excited... that it was over!

The next day, I went to check the signup sheet for people who wanted to help. Scrawled in large letters were the words "Suck cow udder! Go vegan!" Oh, yeah: I had forgotten that some folks in organic farming would reject the idea of drinking milk. My first hater.

The next comment was from a nineteen-year-old girl who said her parents owned a conventional dairy, but she had two organically raised cows of her own, and she wanted to be the first one in Massachusetts to get licensed.

A committee was formed with me, that young farmer, another dairy farmer, and some Harvard grad dude with zero interest in raw milk but with a strong desire to help out a nonprofit for the sake of his résumé, and who wasn't scared to go to Government Center in downtown Boston to petition for our ideas. In the meantime, we built support among farmers and consumers and came up with testing protocols for bacteria levels that went far beyond those required for pasteurized milk and eliminated all concerns for safety. Eighteen months and gallons of shared herbal iced tea later, that farmer girl was the first to be licensed to sell raw milk in the state of Massachusetts. As of this date, there are twenty-eight licensed dairies. I don't drink milk anymore, but I still count that as one of my life's contributions.

That single experience convinced me to rethink speaking as something to be avoided at all costs and instead to see it as a transformational force for change. But you already know that speaking is powerful stuff.

So does Tamsen Webster. Tamsen helps individuals develop their big ideas and teaches organizations how to tell their stories in a way that sticks in the minds of the audience. She was also an executive producer for one of the oldest TEDx stages in the United States and has a busy speaking schedule of her own. After I saw Tamsen give a five-minute talk, I immediately knew I wanted to hire her to help me articulate my own idea about overcoming the fear of speaking, so I could land clients and help them too.

As I worked with her over the months, Tamsen hinted that she was taking notes for herself because she struggled with many of the same things that I had answers for. She used to have a panic disorder, she said, and was often on medication and in and out of therapy for it. It had been ten years since she'd had an attack and been off medication, yet she still had significant anxiety getting onstage. Not that anyone would notice, because she was a good performer. But on the inside, she suffered from nerves.

Tamsen told me, "When I went out onstage at TEDx-Cambridge, I couldn't feel my hands. I accepted the nerves as the way it is for me when I speak, and thought that I'll just have to get used to it. It's a testament to how strongly I believe in the power of speaking—that I would essentially endure this level of anxiety all these years."

When Tamsen saw the possibility of changing her inner experience, though, we traded roles and I coached her. It was more than the anxiety that bothered her. She was usually brought in as a breakout speaker. Breakout sessions are those side events at a conference where you can learn about specific topics. She used to have a dream of being a keynoter as well, the mainstage speaker who addressed all the attendees at the open or close of the event. But it was these keynote talks that made her most nervous, especially when she used new material. She told me maybe she just wasn't cut out to be a keynoter. I told her maybe she was or maybe she wasn't, but she wouldn't know the truth of that until she got over her nerves.

After several sessions, I received an email from Tamsen.

"I did my new 'interactive' keynote last week and it felt *great*. Wasn't nervous onstage at all. And it was fun... and funny! Yay!"

If you think this work changed the trajectory of Tamsen's career, you're right. I caught up with her a few years later when I invited her on my TV show, *Women Inspired*.

She shared, "Since working with you, my nervousness is completely gone. And that's allowed me to be more thoroughly myself onstage and have fun! I used to feel as if I were two different people, one onstage and another person off. Now I'm the same person wherever I speak. I'm really proud of that."

Just writing out these words brings tears to my eyes. You, seeing her onstage excited to be with her audience.

But it didn't end there for Tamsen. "I've seen results in my speaking career too," she said. "It's been really fun how my evaluations as a speaker have dramatically gone up as well as requests for me to keynote. All from overcoming my nerves."

Maybe you want the same results as Tamsen—to be a sought-after and well-paid keynoter. Or your dreams may be entirely different. You may want to speak up at town meetings to help the church in your historic town center get permission to install solar panels. Or you might want to promote your new software or service, or be seen as a leader at work, or you want to love speaking to your managers and employees.

Now you have the tools to uncover and clear away those things that have been holding you back. Now you have the practices that make expressing yourself fun and that expand your self-awareness, and you know how to appreciate the specialness of each present moment in the limelight.

You've begun the journey, so keep with the momentum. Don't let yourself slide back into your old patterns of playing small and hiding away. There will be invitations and possibilities that present themselves to you. I want you to be ready for them.

You will show up, right? I mean, look at what you've already done. You've read this entire book. (Thank you very much, from the bottom of my heart!) Overcoming your fear of being seen is but one leg of your journey to realize your dreams. If you have made this commitment to yourself, you will get to where you want to go. It's a matter of when—in two years, five, ten, or right now.

Here's what I want you to keep in the front of your mind: the sooner you set yourself free, the more time you get to hang out with yourself on the other side of fear with all the benefits it brings.

You are an amazing human being. When you release what is holding you back and open up your free self-expression, you'll get to revel in that sunbeam. How fantastic that will feel when you cut the cords that bind you! When you step beyond those jittery nerves and worries and into that steadfast confidence, where speaking and expressing yourself is one of your favorite things to do. You are meant to express yourself in your totally unique way and delight in the lime-light, just as the child delights in expressing herself.

What now? Are you done? I'm amazed by how confident and clear clients are on the other side of fear. Of course, everyone is different. Maria, the company editor we heard about earlier, said that after that very first webinar training she gave, her fear completely disappeared. Tamsen Webster says she does feel butterflies now and again for a minute or two. A few butterflies are fine. Even my friend and brand advisor Terri Trespicio, who claims she's never met a mic she didn't like, says that her mouth gets dry sometimes. The point is, you don't want the physical symptoms to take up any mental bandwidth or impede your ability to be present and rockin' out your spotlight moments.

When I googled way back when how to get over my nerves and came across the idea of reframing nerves as excitement, the concept was beyond me. Now, I under-stand how that might work. I think this is what Tamsen and Terri do. Studies show that a little bit of cortisol can actually increase your brain focus. Here's the thing: quantity mat-ters. A little bit of salt in a recipe makes it yummy, while too much salt ruins the dish. Likewise, a bit of cortisol favorably increases your brain focus, but too much will have the oppo-site effect and shut down parts of your brain. Those passing butterflies in your tummy, or dry mouth, that little bit of cor-tisol, may be the quantity that you can reframe as excitement, if it feels true and easy to do.

It also can happen that after you've cleared the fear and you are enjoying your newfound freedom, a new and fantas-tic opportunity comes your way to speak on TV, in a sport arena, or to a roomful of C-suite execs in ties, and suddenly you're the kid again being brought into the principal's office. When you have this fantastic new opportunity, and you will, you will also have the Inner Freedom Framework to help you declutter that as-yet unvisited corner in your psychic closet.

I'm super-proud of and impressed by you. By reading this book, you took a giant step toward your dreams. What many people don't realize is, when you ignore your fear of being seen or put off finding your confidence until everything else is in place, you hamper your progress and put off reaching your goals. When you declutter the psychic closet, release self-criticism, and give yourself permission to explore, expressing yourself becomes comfortable and fun.

This comfort leads you to believe in and appreciate yourself each step of the way. You'll allow yourself to love the process of improvement, starting with the "sloppy first draft" to the polished product. It means living your life as an enjoyable creative process. It's worth it and it *is* possible.

As you heal the past and step into the present, ready for your future without excess baggage, you will suddenly see more possibilities for yourself than you could imagine before. The world will open up in new and unexpected ways.

This work of overcoming your fear of speaking is nothing less than a fight for your true self to emerge. Because that's what you find on the other side of fear. You find *you*! You, uninhibited. You, fearlessly sharing your opinion without concern of rejection. You, excited to *be* with your audience, and discovering your delight in the limelight.

ACKNOWLEDGMENTS

A LOUD SHOUTOUT TO the universe for the journey it has sent me on. As I look back, I see how the dots connect and embrace it all.

To my husband, partner, and friend, Endre: Thank you for your enduring love and admiration, and for your interest in and long conversations about all the topics in this book.

To my daughter, Lexi, for showing me what it looks like to love your voice and freely express yourself. I learn so much from you.

Thank you to my sisters, Judith and Susan, who still love me, even though I "told on them."

To Dad: If you were around today, you'd be so proud, even if you never actually read the book. And Mom: You never had an introspective bone in your body, but you gave me a lot of great stories. You always did love a great story.

Susan Robbins, you were my initial inspiration to sing. You got me started and on the stage. My understanding of and many of my core beliefs about performance energy were inspired by you. Thank you. And thank you to all my singing sisters in Libana. Together, we traveled the world in music and performance. The ripples from those experiences informed many of my ideas here.

Thank you, Tatiana Sarbinska, for "making me" work on my speaking voice in our singing lessons. You opened up a new path on my journey.

Thank you, Charlotte Russell, for helping me deconstruct my vocal anatomy, parts of speech, and vocal production through Estill Voice Training.

Thank you, Eliza Bergeson, who when I was starting off my online entrepreneurial journey said, "I love your stage presence, Linda. Maybe you could help people with your stage presence." It turned out you were right.

Thank you to Darius Mozafarian, who first modeled what delight looks like in a grown-up. We are dancing partners from afar, and snowflakes of what I learned from you adorn these pages.

Thank you, Rebecca Henderson, who went before me on this roller coaster ride of authorship. You modeled persistence, excellence, and companionship.

Thank you, Suzanne Kingsbury, who through Gateless Writing taught me to love the words on the page.

Thank you, AJ Harper, for your guidance, editing, insight, and inspiration, all toward a book that changes people's lives, including my own.

To the team at Page Two, and especially my editor, Amanda Lewis, and copyeditor, Steph VanderMeulen: thank you for the team support that elevated my message and made the process a delight.

To all of my students, clients, and workshop participants, and to you, my dear reader: Thank you for the honor to guide you on this part of your life journey.

NOTES

The Inner Freedom Framework Part 1: Reveal and Heal
"I'm reading this," she said... Elaine Morgan, *The Descent of the Child: Human Evolution from a New Perspective* (London, UK: Souvenir Press, 1994).

2: See Yourself Succeed
Studies back up this idea... "Can Visualizing Your Body Doing Something Help You Learn to Do It Better?" *Scientific American*, May 1, 2015, doi. org/10.1038/scientificamericanmind0515-72a.

3: Review to Reveal
When the participants ruminated on the occurrences... The Hope College study can be read here: Charlotte van Oyen Witvliet, Thomas E. Ludwig, and Kelly L. Vander Laan, "Granting Forgiveness or Harboring Grudges: Implications for Emotion, Physiology, and Health," *Psychological Science* 12, no. 2 (March 2001): 117–23, doi.org/10.1111/1467-9280.00320.

4: Look Inside Your Closet
Suzanne Kingsbury created this process... To learn more about Gateless Writing, go to suzannekingsbury.net/for-writers-only/gateless-writing/.

5: Heal What You Reveal
Numerous controlled studies have shown... You can read more about this in this article: Linda Geronilla et al., "EFT (Emotional Freedom Techniques) Remediates PTSD and Psychological Symptoms in Veterans: A Randomized Controlled Replication Trial," *Energy Psychology Journal*, doi.org/10.9769/EPJ.2016.8.2.LG.

According to University of Texas psychologist... James W. Pennebaker and Cindy Chung, "Expressive Writing, Emotional Upheavals, and Health," *Foundations of Health Psychology*, ed. H. S. Friedman and R. C. Silver (New York: Oxford University Press, 2007), 263–84.

6: Transform the Inner Critic

Several years ago, I did some research... See Christopher Peterson and Martin Seligman, *Character Strengths and Virtues: A Handbook and Classification* (Washington and New York: American Psychological Association and Oxford University Press, 2004). You may also read the book here: teachingpsychology.files.wordpress.com/2011/11/character-strengths-and-virtues.pdf.

In her book Playing Big*...* Tara Mohr, *Playing Big: Practical Wisdom for Women Who Want to Speak Up, Create, and Lead* (New York: Avery, 2015).

7: Heal Your Self-Image

The study found that self-criticism... Theodore Powers, Richard Koestner, and David Zuroff, "Self-Criticism, Goal Motivation, and Goal Progress," *Journal of Social and Clinical Psychology* 26, no. 7 (2007): 826–40, doi.org/10.1521/jscp.2007.26.7.826.

There is a video on YouTube... Dothetest, "Test Your Awareness: Do the Test," March 10, 2008, YouTube video, 1:08, youtube.com/watch?v=Ahg6qcgoay4.

8: The Power of Positive Regard

The premise of Glasser's book is twofold... Howard Glasser and Jennifer Easley, *Transforming the Difficult Child*, 3rd ed. (Tucson: Nurtured Heart Publications, 1999).

In his TEDx *talk "The Validation Paradox. . ."* Jeffrey Shaw, "The Validation Paradox: Finding Your Best Through Others," TEDxLincolnSquare, uploaded by TEDxTalks, May 7, 2018, YouTube video, 12:04, youtube.com/watch?v=pEb5NUu5SnM.

9: Reset Your Mindset

"There are about 3 million notes..." Idina Menzel (@idinamenzel), "This is something I said in an interview a few months ago," Twitter, January 1, 2015, 8:07 p.m., twitter.com/idinamenzel/status/550820768326877185/photo/1.

Michael Port, author of Steal the Show... If you want to learn more about this, check out Michael Port's Heroic Public Speaking Grad program at heroic publicspeaking.com/grad-school.

Steve Solomon is the author of many farming books... Steve Solomon with Erica Reinheimer, *The Intelligent Gardener: Growing Nutrient-Dense Food* (Gabriola Island, BC: New Society Publishers, 2012).

Novelist Jenna Blum promotes her books... I came by this during Jenna Blum's "How to Give a Good Reading" GrubStreet workshop, on October 18, 2019. For more, see grubstreet.org.

In his book Known, *Mark Schaefer suggests...* Known: The Handbook for Building and Unleashing Your Personal Brand in the Digital Age (Schaefer Marketing Solutions, 2017).

Studies say that gratitude activates... Robert Emmons, "Why Gratitude Is Good," *Greater Good Magazine*, November 16, 2010, greatergood.berkeley. edu/article/item/why_gratitude_is_good.

10: Practice Your Confident Presence

This kind of mirroring... Cynthia F. Berrol, "Neuroscience Meets Dance/ Movement Therapy: Mirror Neurons, the Therapeutic Process and Empathy," *The Arts in Psychotherapy* 33, no. 4 (December 2006): 302–15, doi.org/10.1016/j.aip.2006.04.001.

a team of neuroscientists in Parma, Italy... C. Keysers et al., "Audiovisual Mirror Neurons and Action Recognition," *Experimental Brain Research* 153, no. 4 (August 2003): 628–36, doi.org/10.1007/s00221-003-1603-5.

In 2020, when everyone was online... Watch "Jon Stewart Talks Confederate Statues, COVID-19 & Irresistible | The Daily Social Distancing Show," *The Daily Show with Trevor Noah*, June 25, 2020, YouTube video, youtube.com/watch?v=3OC4CIfZ_IA.

11: The Breath You Take and Sounds You Make

In Dr. Ivan Joseph's TEDx talk... Ivan Joseph, "The Skill of Self-Confidence," TEDxRyersonU, uploaded by TEDxTalks, January 13, 2012, YouTube video, 13:20, youtube.com/watch?v=w-HYZv6HzAs.

12: Expressively, Naturally You

Charles Limb studied the brains of jazz improvisers... Charles Limb, "Your Brain on Improv," TEDxMidAtlantic, uploaded by TED-Ed, July 3, 2013, YouTube video, 16:31, youtube.com/watch?v=U4k5JFmahVY.

13: Prepare the Way for the Words You Say

the problem of winging it in order to feel natural... Again, this came from Michael Port's Heroic Public Speaking Grad program. See HPS Grad at heroicpublicspeaking.com/grad-school.

Kit Pang of BostonSpeaks... You can check out Kit, a public speaking coach, at bostonspeaks.com.

Some speakers resist memorization... See Seth Godin's June 18, 2019, post called "Awkward Memorization" on his blog at seths.blog/2019/06/awkward-memorization.

The two most popular memorization hacks... Check out the TED talk by Joshua Foer about mnemonics, as well as his book *Moonwalking with Einstein.* "Feats of Memory Anyone Can Do," TED2012, filmed February 2012, TED video, 20:13, ted.com/talks/joshua_foer_feats_of_memory_anyone_can_do?language=en.

Conclusion

Plus, according to some studies... Here is one of those studies on the benefits of raw milk for allergies: G. Loss et al., "The Protective Effect of Farm Milk Consumption on Childhood Asthma and Atopy: The GABRIELA Study," *Journal of Allergy and Clinical Immunology* 128, no. 4 (2011): 766–73, doi.org/10.1016/j.jaci.2011.07.048.

Studies show that pasteurizing breast milk... See, for example, Indira Narayanan et al., "Randomised Controlled Trial of Effect of Raw and Holder Pasteurised Human Milk and of Formula Supplements on Incidence of Neonatal Infection," *The Lancet* 324, no. 8412 (November 17, 1984): 1111–13, doi.org/10.1016/S0140-6736(84)91554-X.

Today across Europe... Sylvia Onusic, "Fresh Milk, Raw Milk, Anytime at the Mlekomat: Automatic Milk Machines in Slovenian Markets," *Taste of Slovenia* (blog), April 12, 2014, foodtoursslovenia.wordpress.com/2014/04/12/fresh-milk-raw-milk-anytime-at-the-mlekomat-automatic-milk-machine-in-slovenian-markets.

BIBLIOGRAPHY

Anderson, Chris. *TED Talks: The Official TED Guide to Public Speaking.* Boston, MA: Mariner, 2017.

Baer, Jay. *Hug Your Haters: How to Embrace Complaints and Keep Your Customers.* New York: Portfolio, 2016.

Canfield, Jack, with Janet Switzer. *The Success Principles: How to Get from Where You Are to Where You Want to Be.* Rev. ed. New York: William Morrow, 2015.

Faber, Adele, and Elaine Mazlish. *How to Talk so Kids Will Listen & Listen so Kids Will Talk.* Rev. ed. New York: Scribner, 2012.

Foer, Joshua. *Moonwalking with Einstein: The Art and Science of Remembering Everything.* New York: Penguin, 2011.

Gawain, Shakti. *Creative Visualization: Use the Power of Your Imagination to Create What You Want in Your Life.* Rev. ed. Novato, CA: New World Library, 2010.

Gilbert, Elizabeth. *Big Magic: Creative Living Beyond Fear.* New York: Penguin, 2016.

Glasser, Howard, and Jennifer Easley. *Transforming the Difficult Child.* 3rd ed. Tucson: Nurtured Heart Publications, 1999.

Hay, Louise. *Love Your Body: A Positive Affirmation Guide for Loving and Appreciating Your Body.* Rev. ed. Carlsbad, CA: Hay House, 1998.

Hendricks, Gay. *The Big Leap: Conquer Your Hidden Fear and Take Life to the Next Level.* New York: HarperOne, 2010

———. *Conscious Breathing: Breathwork for Health, Stress Release, and Personal Mastery.* New York: Bantam, 1995.

Jones, Phil M. *Exactly What to Say: The Magic Words for Influence and Impact.* Vancouver, BC: Page Two, 2018.

Karia, Akash. *How to Deliver a Great TED Talk: Presentation Secrets of the World's Best Speakers.* Scotts Valley, CA: CreateSpace, 2013.

Katz, Richard. *Boiling Energy: Community Healing Among the Kalahari Kung.* Cambridge, MA: Harvard University Press, 1984.

Lesser, Elizabeth. *Cassandra Speaks: When Women Are the Storytellers, the Human Story Changes.* New York: Harper Wave, 2020.

Liedloff, Jean. *The Continuum Concept: In Search of Happiness Lost.* Boston, MA: Da Capo Press, 1986.

Linklater, Kristin. *Freeing the Natural Voice: Imagery and Art in the Practice of Voice and Language.* Rev. ed. Hollywood, LA: Quite Specific Media, 2006.

Mohr, Tara. *Playing Big: Practical Wisdom for Women Who Want to Speak Up, Create, and Lead.* New York: Avery, 2015.

Morgan, Elaine. *The Descent of the Child: Human Evolution from a New Perspective.* London, UK: Souvenir Press, 1994.

Port, Michael. *Steal the Show: From Speeches to Job Interviews to Deal-Closing Pitches, How to Guarantee a Standing Ovation for All the Performances in Your Life.* Boston, MA: Mariner, 2016.

Port, Michael, and Andrew Davis. *The Referable Speaker: Your Guide to Building a Sustainable Speaking Career—No Fame Required.* Vancouver, BC: Page Two, 2021.

Rogers, C. R. *On Becoming: A Therapist's View of Psychotherapy.* Boston, MA: Houghton Mifflin Harcourt, 1961.

Tolle, Eckhart. *A New Earth: Awakening to Your Life's Purpose.* Rev. ed. New York: Penguin, 2008.

———. *The Power of Now: A Guide to Spiritual Enlightenment.* Novato, CA: New World Library, 2004.

Voss, Chris. *Never Split the Difference: Negotiating as if Your Life Depended on It.* New York: Harper Business, 2016.

Webster, Tamsen. *Find Your Red Thread: Make Your Big Ideas Irresistible.* Vancouver, BC: Page Two, 2021.

Westney, William. *The Perfect Wrong Note: Learning to Trust Your Musical Self.* Lanham, MD: Amadeus, 2006.